Chennai and Coimbatore, India

Vincenzo Berghella

Copyright Page

Copyright year: 2018

ISBN No: 978-0-578-20085-9

From the same author:

- **Obstetric Evidence Based Guidelines.** Informa Healthcare, London, UK, and New York, USA (2007) [English]

- **Maternal Fetal Evidence Based Guidelines.** Informa Healthcare, London, UK, and New York, USA (2007) [English]

- **Laughter, the best medicine. Jokes for everyone.** (2007) [English]

- **Ridere, la migliore medicina. Barzellette per bambini.** (2007) [Italiano]

- **My favorite quotes.** (2009) [English]

- **In medio stat virtus – Citazioni d'autore.** (2009) [Italiano]

- **Quello che di voi vive in me.** (2009) [Italiano]

- **Dall'altra parte dell'oceano.** (2010) [Italiano] (Translated in: **On the other side of the ocean.** (2013) [English])

- **Preterm Birth: Prevention and Management.** Wiley-Blackwell. Oxford, United Kingdom. (2010) [English]

- **From father to son.** (2010) [English]

- **Sollazzi.** (2010) [Italiano]

- **The land of religions.** (2011) [English] (Translated in: **La terra delle religioni.** (2013) [Italiano])

- **Giramondo.** (2011) [Italiano]

- **Obstetric Evidence Based Guidelines.** Informa Healthcare, London, UK, and New York, USA (2012; Second Edition) [English]

- **Maternal Fetal Evidence Based Guidelines.** Informa Healthcare, London, UK, and New York, USA (2012; Second Edition) [English]
- **Trip to London.** (2012) [English]
- **Il primo amore non si scorda mai.** (2012) [Italiano]
- **Maldives.** (2013) [English]
- **Russia.** (2013) [English]
- **Happiness: the scientific path to achieving wellbeing.** (2014) [English] (Translated in **Felicita': il percorso scientifico per raggiungere il benessere** [Italian])
- **New Zealand: 100% pure.** (2014) [English]
- **Me dentro: i primi scritti dai 17 ai 20 anni** (2015) [Italiano]
- **Me dentro: alla ricerca dell'amore** (2015) [Italiano]

- **US Rowing Youth Nationals** (2015) [English]

- **Polynesia** (2016) [English]

- **Obstetrics: Normal and Problem Pregnancies** (Gabbe, Niebyl, Simpson, Landon, Galan, Janiaus, Driscoll, Berghella, Grobman). Elsevier, Philadelphia, USA (2016; Seventh Edition) [English]

- **Obstetric Evidence Based Guidelines.** CRC Press, London, UK, and New York, USA (2017; Third Edition) [English]

- **Maternal Fetal Evidence Based Guidelines.** CRC Press, London, UK, and New York, USA (2017; Third Edition) [English]

- **Operative Obstetrics.** (Apuzzio, Vintzileos, Berghella, Alvarez-Perez) CRC Press, London, UK, and New York, USA (2017; Fourth Edition) [English]

- **Krakow and Auschwitz.** (2017) [English]

- **Barcelona.** (2018) [English]

- **M'zav, Algeria**. (2018) [English]

- **Labor and Delivery: Evidence Based Management.** (Berghella, Saccone, Ghi, Roman) JayPee Brothers, India (2018) [English]

Dedicated to all my Indian friends, among them (but not only) Sulagna Chakraborty Saitta (from Kolkata), Rupsa Chaudhuny Boelig (from Kolkata), Sushma Jwala (from Hyderabad), Priya Koduri (from Hyderabad), Priya Mammen (from Kerala), Reshama Saralkar Navathe (from Mumbai), Anju Suhag (from Rohtak, Haryana, North India) and Srini - Padmanabhan Srinivasan (from Chennai).

Why India

I've been fascinated by India and the South East since I was a young child. The first books I read with passion when I was 12, 13, 14 years old, were about Sandokan. Sandokan was a fictional pirate of the late 19th century, who first appeared in publication in 1883, created by Italian author Emilio Salgari.

He is the protagonist of eleven adventure novels, and I read them all. He was dark, strong, invincible, and had plenty of women. I definitively dreamed to be like him. I have been told I look like Sandokan, and even more times I've been told I look Indian.

As I got just a tiny bit older, the first real non-fiction book I read was Freedom at midnight, by Lapierre and Collins. These masterful journalists narrated the quest for independence of India, which was eventually successful on August 15, 1947.

Another idol of mine was heavily mentioned and described in these pages: Mahatma Gandhi. This time the hero was even more impressive, as Gandhi was a true immense figure of history, who changed the world. Stanotte la liberta' (I read the book in Italian, of course) remains one of my favorite books ever.

We love Indian food. While I'm lucky enough to have lived for over 23 years with one of the best cooks I've ever met, the few times we order out, or go out for dinner, Indian is what Paola and I go for. Indian food is simply delicious, we love its spiciness, its being based on vegetables, its tasteful sauces, its easy digestion. Eating Indian is often close to an orgasmic experience for me.

Indians are also so many of my good friends and professional colleagues, as I stated at the start of this book. I have been fascinated not only by their good looks, but even more by their smartness and determination.

My invitation to go and talk in India came, as usual, by happenstance. During my year as President of the Society for Maternal-Fetal Medicine (SMFM), I pushed for greater global collaboration of our US-based high-risk-pregnancy society with other similar societies worldwide. I became the head of its International Members taskforce.

Our successful expansion also attracted the interest of Asha Rijhsinghani, an Indian maternal-fetal medicine specialist who now works in Albany, NY, but who is originally from Mumbai. It soon became apparent she was passionate about helping expand the SMFM brand in India, where she knows pretty much everyone who counts in our field.

We spoke for quite a while at the luncheon for International Members I helped organize at the 37th Annual Congress of SMFM in Las Vegas in January, 2017. I had been invited months prior in 2016 to a conference in India later in 2017, but had not yet made reservations. Asha's suggestion was that if SMFM was serious about reaching out to Asia's subcontinent, I needed to go there. I immediately agreed to the plan.

Over the next few weeks and months, dozens of emails were exchanged through not just Asha and I, but many others, whose Indian names were unknown to me. Taken by so many other duties and interests, I went with the flow, agreeing to whatever plans were being made. SMFM had agreed to send me, and someone in India would pay for my ticket. I did not look much at details.

The only thing I knew is that the main congress I was to attend and speak at was in Chennai, the former Madras, in South India. And that from there I would have a short trip to Coimbatore, too, where another conference had been organized. All I did initially was to add those days in my calendar, and let my trusted, wonderful assistant Lynn block my schedule for a few days.

As time went by, I realized I was going to have a very busy end of July 2017, as I was due for an SMFM Board meeting in Toronto on July 19-23, 2017, and our annual summer family vacation in Italy would also have to be at the end of July and beginning of August.

I first booked the trip Philadelphia-Toronto-Rome-Philadelphia. Inside it, so to speak, leaving from Rome, I booked the trip to India. It was not easy. Via Expedia, I found Emirates flights from Rome to Dubai, and then from Dubai to Chennai, and viceversa.

The head of the congress in Chennai, Gita Arjun, was adamant I arrive a day ahead before the conference, to avoid any problems with plane delays or cancellations. So my first legs of the trip were leaving Rome on Thursday July 27th, to arrive in Chennai at 2:40am on Friday the 28th. This would be more than 24 hours ahead of my talk, scheduled in Chennai on Saturday July 29th.

The organizers of the Coimbatore conference told me they would book the Chennai-Coimbatore flight for me and Asha. So that was the one thing I would not worry about. Then I had to organize the flights back to Rome from Coimbatore.

I looked at several options. Asha suggested I fly from Coimbatore to Mumbai, then to Rome. But these options were difficult regarding airlines, times and costs. Finally I found the option to go back from Coimbatore to Chennai, then to Dubai, then to Rome, the most efficient and feasible one.

And so I booked the two fights Rome-Dubai, Dubai-Chennai, and the three going back, Coimbatore-Chennai, Chennai-Dubai, Dubai-Rome, with one Expedia reservation. I was now heading to India!!

The trip was going to be a short one, but I was so excited about it anyway. I have traveled a lot, and I know that even a 24-hour trip can be unforgettable. In the last nine months, my two-day trip to Krakow and Auschwitz, and three-day trip to Barcelona, both generated books of over a hundred pages each.

Given how busy I am with all other activities at work and at home, I begin to concentrate on the trip just during the last week. Earlier in the month, from July 3rd to 8th, I was in Algeria, an unforgettable experience. Only after that is over, I go and buy a couple of travel books about South India. I review past emails to see exactly what are the plans, in particular the titles of my talks in each conference.

I'm supposed to talk twice on July 29 in Chennai at the PROGRESS meeting; and twice on July 30 in Coimbatore at the Women Center meeting. I prepare the slides, all on topics I adore and I am well versed in: prevention of preterm birth, and how to do a cesarean delivery.

Given I'll be over three weeks away, and visit three continents, my packing is a bit more complex than usual. I have to pack converter plugs for Canada, Italy, and South India. I need elegant clothes for the meetings and conferences, as well as bathing suits and flip-flops. I better make sure I have all my equipment for riding on a plane, I'll be flying quite a bit...

I get to Toronto no problem, from there back to Philadelphia, where I enjoy my layover at the airport in the VIP lounges of American Airlines and then also British Airways, enjoying quality time with my friend Marco, who is also leaving for Europe. Once in Italy, I spend a day in Tarquinia with my in-laws, and a couple of days with my parents in Pescara. All are well, considering they are all pretty much in their 80's.

I check in online my India flights. At least the first two ones, Rome-Dubai and Dubai-Chennai, for July 27th, 2017. I'm supposed to take off at 11:30am on the 27th from Fiumicino, and land in Chennai at 2:45am on the 28th. I'm getting pretty excited. So are my counterparts in India.

Thursday July 27, 2017

With just a carry-on and a new leather black bag with laptop, documents, chargers and airplane items (headphones, eyecover, headcover, water bottle, head rest), I arrive in Fiumicino, leave back my rent-a-car at Avis, and get to Gate 34, for the Emirates flight EK 100 from Rome to Dubai, scheduled to be on-time at 11:30am.

In fact, I get to the gate in plenty of time, since I'm already checked in. I must have arrived at gate 34 two hours early. I enjoy starting to read my travel guides to India, and fantasize about all the interesting places to visit.

My only worry is to keep enough batteries for my laptop, so I can do some work and write on it. But I relax thinking that I have a new powerful recharger, and I imagine I'll probably be able to recharge laptop and iPhone directly on my Emirates seat. They are a great airline, with modern planes and all the comforts. Much better than American Airlines.

As I'm immersed in flow in my writings on my MacBookAir, the Emirates staff at the gate starts announcing updates. I'm glad, we must be getting close to boarding. At some point, they go through a list of passenger names. I've heard these kinds of announcements thousands of times.

But this time I hear, "..., Berghella, ..." What? Did they really say my name? I let them repeat the announcement. "...., Berghella, ..." It's confirmed, it really sounds like my last name. I was not expecting to be upgraded to first class. Maybe my preferred status with American Airline counts something with Emirates as well?

I get to the counter, where three staff officials are waiting. The lady on the right asks for my passport and boarding pass. I hand them over proudly, as I'm confident all is fine. She looks and looks at my passport. Then looks up at me, "Where is the visa?"

"What visa?" I reply dumbly. "You need a visa for India," she states gently. And she is gauging I guess if I'm indeed stupid, ignorant, playing with her, or just a plain fool. I begin to panic. Never imagined I needed a visa for India.

To go to Algeria earlier this month, I had worked hard with the help of my friend Daoud Ouladaoud to get a visa for Algeria. Algeria is the kind of country you need a visa for. But India! Come on! These are the nicest people, a peaceful country, there are so many Indians in the US.

But the Emirates official is serious. The one next to her now is looking at us, since a potentially important issue has been uncovered. I try to go to plan B, as I know I have no visa at all. I never thought of it. Nobody ever told me.

"I have an Italian passport, too." I'm sure this will work. Everyone loves Italy. Why would India require a visa for Italians? I spend a second or two of wonderful bliss thinking my Plan B is for sure going to work.

"Sorry, you need a visa for India with a US or an Italian passport," the official tells me softly. They are not mean, they are just doing their job. They seem somewhat incredulous I do not know that. "We cannot let you fly to Dubai, as your ticket is linked to Chennai, so you cannot board this plane without an Indian visa."

I start to panic inside a bit. I remain very calm outside. The third Emirates official moves closer to us. He is clearly the supervisor. He is even more kind, "So sorry, but a visa is needed for India." "How do I get one??" I begin to ask myself.

It's pretty clear I will not get a visa in a few minutes. The flight is leaving in less than 45 minutes. I will need to also reschedule both flights, the Rome-Dubai and the Dubai-Chennai. I ask the staff officials if they could change my flights there at the gate, or if I should go to the Emirates counter at Terminal 3.

They check my ticket carefully. "We at Emirates cannot change your tickets. You bought them through a third party. They would be the ones to change the tickets." Oh my. That's right, I bought my tickets through Expedia. I know the rules of air travel well. They are correct. Another hurdle.

I move myself away from the counter. I'm not the only customer. About 800 people are about to board the huge Emirates flight to Dubai. And it looks like I won't be able to. It feels to me like I'm having an out-of-body experience. I'm temporarily defeated, but not broken. Someone's character is best judged by moments of difficulty.

I start working with my iPhone frantically. I google "Visa for India." Google is the eternal savior these days, isn't it? I find a 'visaforindia' site which claims I can get an emergency visa. The first option is for 48 hours turnaround. Well, by then the conference I'm supposed to speak at would have started already. Too late.

I check again. This seems to be a reliable site. There is an option to get the visa, paying more money, in about 24 hours. Still a bit late. I figure I should try to rebook the same flights for the 28th, the next day, to have any luck to arrive on time to give my first two talks. The first is the bigger conference.

In fact, I would miss the first meeting, scheduled for the 28th for dinner, with 35 Indian ob-gyn physicians who are flying into Chennai apparently just to meet me, and to discuss how to collaborate with SMFM. If I leave 24 hours late, I would get in Chennai at 2:45am the 29th. At least on time for my talks, which would start at 10:20am. The dinner meeting on the 28th is impossible to make.

I inform via WhatsApp Asha, who is already in India. I figure I am not only missing the first meeting, but I could probably miss all talks in both congresses. I better let them know sooner rather than later, so they can make arrangements.

I feel really sad. I really wanted to go. They - in India - had prepared so much for me. SMFM had counted on me to market the society in the subcontinent. Personally, my whole trip this summer was organized around going to India. I would feel guilt taking three weeks off in Italy without doing some work.

I continue frantically working on my iPhone. The 'visaforindia' site is easy to work with. I find another option, the quickest one: 5 hours to get a visa to India. I enter lots of information from my passport, and credit card. And submit what I can gather. This looks like my best emergency option for now.

I have nothing else I can do here at the gate. As passengers board 'my' plane, I walk back out of this area. In almost 40 years of international air travel (I was 15 when I first flew commercially, Bologna to London, in 1979), I had never before had to exit a boarding gate area.

I retrace my steps. I go down the escalator I went up hundreds of times in the last few decades. I take the train back to the check-in areas, in a car all by myself. It does not feel real. But I'm alive, and well, and determined to improve what looks like a impossible-to-fix, sad situation.

Obviously I need to change the tickets. So I head to the Emirates counter. There is no line. A nice man confirms what I had already heard. I need to call the third party who sold me the tickets. I do not know why they never state the name 'Expedia.' They must hate them? Unfair competition? He is nice, anyways, and I know he is correct.

I find a quiet seat in front of the Emirates check-in counters, and start working. I have my iPhone, my laptop connected to internet via my iPhone hot spot, and a charger. I should be operational for hours, if needed.

In the meanwhile, I got several WhatsApp messages and emails from India. In particular, someone called 'Mala,' informed by Asha, is trying to find a way to get me an emergency visa. As I am in Rome, she is trying to work with the India Embassy in Rome.

I call Expedia. I have the number, the reservation number, and the airline confirmation numbers for all five flights. I do not have to wait too long to get a live person to help me. Her accent sounds Indian. She seems nice.

At first she states I should change my tickets via Emirates. I convince her quickly that I have tried, and they won't. She tells me there will be at least a $200 change fee. I accept. Between each new question and decision, I often have to wait about five minutes on hold. But she always comes back.

While talking to her, I'm also checking messages and emails. Mala, who I assume is an Indian administrator well versed in getting visas for India, keeps on sending me updates. At some point, she says an Indian Government Undersecretary is working on getting me a visa. Wow!!

I suggest to the Expedia operator to look and try to see if I can change the tickets for the next day, the 28th, on exactly the same flights as today, the 27th. I wait a few minutes on hold again. Then she comes back live. "It's $1,600 plus for the change."

"No way," I think within myself. I did not pay that much for the whole five flights. There must be another way. How can they cost so much? "Unfortunately tomorrow's flights are full, so I can only get you on only with business seats," she states politely. I beg her to look for other options. I stay a few more minutes on hold.

In the meanwhile I check on Expedia online. I find one way tickets to Chennai from Rome for a bit over $600. I guess this will be option B, if the operator does not find me cheaper routes. I'm afraid though that all these tickets won't connect to each other. What if the fact that I did not take today's flights will automatically cancel my return flights, too? This is the industry norm, after all.

I'm also concerned that I might not get the visa on time to board the flights tomorrow. The 'visaforindia' site had sent me several emails – which reassured me they really existed – stating that my visa would be issued at 8am India time on July 28th, 2017, if I provided all needed documents.

I had googled India time, and my calculations were that 8am in India would correspond to 11:30am in Rome. So even if I could change the plane, Emirates staff would not let me board for an 11:30am departure without a visa beforehand. Would they just accept the 'promise' of me getting the visa while in takeoff? Probably not, I guess, they would want a visa BEFORE boarding, at least by 10:30am.

So... would I then need to change tickets again? I guess through another long phone call with Expedia? And another $ penalty? This is getting pretty complicated, I start thinking. I might never be able to get the visa on time to take flights early enough so not to miss my talks.

While on the phone with Expedia, I'm multitasking big way. The 'visaforindia' emails request more information. They want a passport picture, and a picture of my US passport. I'm at the airport, how will I manage all this?

I hope they accept photos from my iPhone, that's the best I can do for now. I take a selfie. I take a picture of my US passport, as elegantly and officially as I can. I send them to my email via iPhone. Then I email them from my laptop. I feel I have created an efficient office.

Mala from India also requests a picture of me, and an official photo of my Italian passport. I also give her the information that I'm working with 'visaforindia,' and she says she will check that route too. Wow. She seems to be working full time on this. I feel blessed to have so many trying to help me out. Asha is sending me updates every few minutes, too.

In the meanwhile, Expedia continues to look for other options for my flights. I'm a bit afraid now that I could book new flights on the phone with this nice Expedia operator, only to find myself without a visa to go anyway. The operator is patient. She talks to her supervisors. She takes my cell number just in case we get disconnected.

Mala emails me she needs now scanned photos of my passports. The ones I sent her are not clear enough. She says I should be able to find a scanner somewhere. Perhaps through Emirates. Wow. Another task. Still keeping on the telephone line with Expedia, I pack up – I loved this little office I had created for myself – and head for the nearby Emirates desk.

The Emirates official knows me from earlier. "No, we cannot do any scanning here, but the airport Information Desk will", and he points to his right, my left, to the immense Fiumicino crowd. I'm not too pleased. But I've got no other option for now.

The Information Desk is less than 100 yards away, not bad. There is only one person in front of me. The officials here seem eager to help, with friendly faces. "Sure, we can scan your documents". Wow, I'm happy. I hand the friendly young lady both my US and my Italian passports. She takes them to the back of the office.

"I hope she does not disappear", I think within myself, worried my documents might disappear. She appears within a minute or so. "Tutto fatto, ecco qui", and she hands me back the passports. I had given her my email. I check it, and there are indeed emails already in my inbox with the two scanned passports. Wow. This was much easier than I thought.

While still on hold with Expedia, I head back with bag, carry-on, passports etc to where I was sitting previously, my new office in Fiumicino Airport. The Expedia operator gives me a new choice. She found I would pay 'just' a bit over $400 by leaving the 28th but a little later, at 3:25pm. After the stop-over in Dubai, I would get into Chennai at 8:20am on the 29th.

After thinking no good option was available, this does not sound too bad. I cannot leave today without a visa anyway. If truly I get the visa from visaforindia at 11:30am Rome time tomorrow, it would give me time to then check-in with Emirates with a visa in hand.

The arrival at 8:20am on the 29th is a bit late, but my talks do not start until 10:30am or so. So I might make them. Or perhaps they could be moved just a bit to give me enough time to clear customs, get from airport to the hotel, where I know the conference is.

There are still many unknowns. Will I really get the visa? Will my new planes be on time? Will I miss the second flight if the first is delayed? Will the customs take forever? Will someone still be able to pick me up at the airport? How far will the hotel be from the airport? I know Chennai is the 4th biggest city in India (after Mumbai, Kolkata, and New Delhi), with up to about 7 million people.

I decide to go for it. I do have the biggest worry of not getting the visa, but I decide to say "yes" to the Expedia operator when she gives me this new option. Then I think, "No, perhaps I should wait for Mala to assure me that I will indeed get a visa", as she is working hard on it.

Mala has been working all her connections in India. Her only trouble has been reaching the Indian Embassy in Rome, in particular their visa desk, which does not seem to be answering. She cannot understand why.

In the meanwhile, my Expedia operator is getting a bit antsy at my indecision. I'm also thinking I could call Expedia later with visa in hand, or book new flights by myself online. The operator tells me this deal might not be available later on.

My calculation in my head is that I would loose just a bit over $400 by rebooking with the Expedia operator. She assures me the return flights would then also be confirmed, and all 5 flights would remain as one reservation, linked to each other. So I agree. I do not really have better options.

The Expedia operator still has to check with supervisors, get me seats, and accept my credit card. Mala in the meanwhile is suggesting perhaps I could go to the Indian Embassy in Rome to try to get an emergency visa. She states that they have been instructed to give me a visa right away, through special government dispensation. But she still has not talked with the visa people at the Rome India Embassy yet, so she does not tell me to go yet.

The phone call with Expedia, when we are all done, has lasted one hour and thirty-five minutes. Wow. I hope after all this I can take off tomorrow afternoon. I guess now I have to figure out what to do. I suppose the first thing is to rent a car.

As I'm packing again my office away from office in Fiumicino airport, I ponder the options for how to spend the next 20 or so hours. Go back to Tarquinia and my family and in-laws? Spend the day in Rome, trying to hook up to the many friends I have who live here? Or go back to Pescara to see my parents and siblings?

But a better option, a brilliant one, comes to my mind. Andrea, our oldest son, is in Naples!! With my excellent friend and colleague Gabriele Saccone, with whom Andrea and his girlfriend Alice are staying!! Naples is only about a two hour drive from Rome. I should be able to make it.

I head to the rent-a-car zone of the Rome Fiumicino Airport, where I have been in the past probably a hundred times. The place is packed. Avis has a huge line, I pick up number 56, and they are still serving number 43. I sit down and try to see if I can book a car online.

Then I notice the Europcar desk has only one person in line. Once I get to an officer, she tells me they really have run out of cars. "Ma comunque, dove dovrebbe andare, lontano? Per quanti giorni?" I state I'll stay around Rome, and keep the car only less than 24 hours. "Le va bene una macchina piccola allora?" Would you mind a small car then? I'm in business!

As I step to Garage B to get the rent-a-car, Mala texts me again saying I should probably head to the Indian Embassy in Rome anyway. She cannot be sure 100% I'll get the US visa from visaforindia site, and she tells me it would be prudent to get one on my Italian passport.

As I drive off the airport, another brilliant idea comes to my mind. The answer to why Mala is not able to communicate with the visa desk at the Indian Embassy in Rome dawns on me. It might be closed!! This is Italy after all.

I stop on the emergency right lane in the highway right after I exit the airport. On my iPhone, I check the Indian Embassy in Rome website. The visa desk? It's open only from 9:30am to

11:30am. It's almost 2pm. That is why Mala has been unable to talk with them.

I call Mala in India. I explain that the visa desk is closed. She advices then to avoid the trip into congested Rome downtown. She tells me she'll keep an eye on the email I should get from visaforindia, which should arrive at 4:30am.

4:30am? I had done my calculations wrong. India time is EARLIER than Italy time. So Mala advises me to wait to hear about the US visa early tomorrow morning. If there would be any problem with the US visa, then I should head into Rome tomorrow morning and try to get the Indian visa in Rome. Great plan! And I'm off to Naples!!

By 5pm, I'm in Naples, and spend an enchanting late afternoon and evening with my beloved son Andrea. I almost get emotional seeing how happy he is to see me. I have not seen him for a little over a month. He is the perfect son. As is Pietro, of course.

The decision is only: stay in Naples overnight and leave early, or head back to Rome or Tarquinia tonight? The company in Naples is great, and Gabriele offers to host me at his home where Andrea is staying. How can I say no?

We walk along the gulf of Naples, we have the biggest gelato - Coppa Amore at Ciro di Mergellina, one of the most famous bars in Naples - I've ever head, we later have pizza with Gabriele's whole family in a nice restaurant. What more can one wish for? I've made the most from a difficult situation. I still hope to be able to leave for India tomorrow. For now, I have lived the present as best as I could.

Friday July 28, 2017

At 6:30am the next morning, after sleeping in Gabriele's parents' nice living room, I see the desired email: my visa to India. I forward the email to Mala. She confirms this is indeed the official visa. Gabriele prints it for me.

By 8:30am, after spending more quality time at breakfast with Andrea and friends, I'm off driving back to Fiumicino, as Andrea and Alice leave at the same time for the Amalfi coast. Life is grand. Never give up; always look at the bright side.

I give the rent-a-car back to Europcar, and I'm at the Emirates check-in desk before they even open. I wait patiently. I make sure I'm the first in line. The official checks my documents. The visa is fine. She prints me two new boarding passes, Rome-Dubai, and Dubai-Chennai. I'm going!!!

By now, many ob-gyns in India know I'll make it to the congresses. I get a lot of 'safe travels' messages from the subcontinent. My blood pressure probably comes down a few millimeters of mercury. I'm the first one to board the economy class on the plane. I'm more than happy to switch seats to allow a newlywed couple to seat together.

I love traveling. I do some work on the plane. We at Jefferson are trying to hire new maternal-fetal medicine attendings in our division. I answer more emails, WhatsApp and text messages. To my surprise, there is wi-fi on the humongous plane, an Airbus A380, double-deck, wide-body, four engine jet.

Maybe having the capability to get and send messages is a bad thing. I try to avoid it. I'm in a comfortable seat. A kid and his mother seat next to me. A parent gives so much to a child. She takes his shoes off; even has a blanket for him. They speak Russian, but a mother is a mother in any language. I think that 99% of people in the world are good. I love life. The almost six hour flight goes by quickly.

Saturday July 29, 2017

I board the Dubai-Chennai flight without any problems. I have a bit less than six more hours, and then I'll be in India!! This is an overnight flight, which leaves at about 3:20am Dubai time, and arrives at 8:20am India time in Chennai,.

I only sleep about two hours in this last flight. I'm a bit cramped. And probably too excited, too. I am finally flying over the subcontinent! I take a picture from the plane of the sandy beach of Chennai. From up here, we could be arriving in my home town of Pescara, which also has a long sandy beach. But I bet things will be a bit different here in South India…

Chennai Airport is not as modern and futuristic as Dubai's. I go to the passport control line, and after less than ten precious minutes – they are waiting for me at the Progress Congress! – I am in front of a friendly Indian official.

"Do you have an e-visa?" He asks me. At first I do not understand his subcontinent accent. Then he repeats himself, showing me back the printed visa I had given him with my US passport. "I guess I do", I answer dumbly. "This is the wrong line. You have to go back there to the e-visa lines".

Dam! I lost a few precious minutes. I had seen nobody in the other line for visas, and assumed they were closed. Now there are a couple of people in front of me. I wait patiently in line. In the meanwhile, about 15 other passengers line behind me; they also had gone to the wrong line. I do not feel as dumb as I did a few minutes earlier.

The two officers in the e-visa counter look a bit stern. They are asking lots of questions to the travelers ahead of me. They are taking their photos. Their fingerprints. But when I am up, the quiet officer, the more junior of the two, does not ask me any questions, and stamps my passport in good time, after checking my visa, my passport, my photo, and my finger-prints. I made it!!

I was able to keep both bag and carry-on with me the whole time. So I head to the exit. It's really warm as I step into Chennai's morning. Humid. A nice young Indian lady has my name, 'Dr Vincenzo Berghella, USA' on a banner. Yes! My savior. India, here I come!!

She is very friendly, with a soft smile. She explains to me there were heavy rains last night, I was lucky to avoid them. That is why it's so humid this morning. Despite being only before 9am, the rain has already mostly evaporated. The light gray seemingly new Mercedes we step into has great air-conditioning. The driver is on the right, British style.

The pre-British history of Chennai and its state, Tamil Naru, is complex and convoluted. In the 3rd century BC, the Sagam age started, and its great literature. Several dynasties followed, until the Pallayas took over in the 7th century. The Cholas ruled in medieval times. By the late 14th century the Vijayanagar Empire ruled Tamil Nadu. These are just names to you reader, but there is so much history and so many legends about these fascinating old times of South India.

Europeans first landed on Tamil's shores in the 16th century. The Portuguese arrived first, followed by the Dutch, the British, the French, and the Danes. Eventually it came down to the British, settled in Chennai, and the French, based at Puducherry. The British won the three Carnatic Wars, fought between 1744 and 1763, and so started British dominance of this part of India.

After the Indian rebellion of 1857, the East India Company which had ruled over India for about a century was replaced with direct Crown rule (Queen Victoria at the time) from the British Empire, and the British Raj was born.

India won independence from the British Empire on August 15, 1947. Jawaharlal Nehru became India's first prime minister. In 1956, the States' Reorganization Act divided the South along linguistic lines, into the present-day states of Tamil Nadu, Kerala, Karnataka and Andhra Pradesh. Narendra Madi won the last elections, in 2014, and is the current prime minister.

The 30 or so minutes car trip is my first glimpse at India. There are electric 'tuk tuks' - auto rickshaws - along the road. The traffic is chaotic, nobody seems to follow any rules. Certainly the cars zig zag among themselves, not staying in their lanes.

Happiness!!! This is India!! There are possibly more motorcycles on the roads than cars. The motorcycles are old, often with more than two, up to five people on them.

Interestingly, the flags along the road out of the airport are those of the ruling party in this state. Politics rule here in India! Most bikers are not wearing helmets. Often there are no traffic lines on the road. There are low-income country shacks along the road, and some tropical trees.

The shop signs and advertising billboards are mostly in Tamil. I'm asking lots of questions to the lady who greeted me at the airport, who seats with me in the back of the Mercedes, while the quiet chauffer is driving. I learn that you write Tamil from left to right, like English. It's a very curvy alphabet.

My guide tells me that since this is the weekend - today is Saturday - there is little traffic, so it's taking us only 30 minutes to the Leela Hotel instead of what would usually be 1.5 hours. The main sound of my first minutes in India is the honking from cars and motorcycles. It's continuous. For passing, drivers have to honk to make a lane ahead of themselves.

In fact, many of the yellow tuk tuks taxis have written in their backs 'Honk please.' Honking is encouraged for safety! Obviously sometimes two cars want to get at the same time in the same 'imagined' lane, so the noise gets to louder levels then as both cars honk uncontrollably.

Sometimes the whole road seem to swift, as the one car is passing on the right, and then gets overtaken by another car at the same time on its right, and then this one is being passed by yet another car honking the loudest on the extreme right, often being squeezed against the guardrail.

My guide tells me many cars are made in India, and in fact in Chennai, considered the 'Detroit' of India. Some are local brands, such as Maruti. Ford also has a large factory here. Interestingly, most motorcycles have more than one person in it. Over 99% of the motorbikes are being driven by adult men. If there is a woman in the back seat, many have both legs hanging on one side, and not open legs behind the man as in the West.

Chennai first settlement was a fort, called St George, erected between 1640 and 1653, which constitutes now with the narrow streets and bazaars of George Town the historic hub of the city. Fort St George was really the original starting point from where the British Empire grew here in India. Madras in time became an important naval and commercial center. The city itself was renamed from Madras to Chennai in 1996.

The city of Madras always had a local name right from its inception. It was called Madras by British but it was also called Chennaipattinam by local population. The reason for this name was that land which was purchased by the East India Company to set up the port of Madras was acquired from a Telugu speaking landlord called Chinnappa Naicker.

From that time local people called the city Chennai Pattinam (pattinam in Tamil means city), while the British called it Madras. Madras was the official name and later since it was the capital for the entire South, the South became known as Madras Presidency.

After independence, the Madras presidency was reorganized in four southern states based on languages spoken there, namely Tamil Nadu, Kerala, Andhra Pradesh and Karnataka. The city of Madras still remained the capital of Tamil Nadu.

Later all over India the official names of cities were changed to those used by local population, so that for example Bombay became Mumbai and Calcutta became Kolkata. Tamil politicians also thought of getting some more popular votes by changing the name of the city of Madras to Chennai.

However the name Chennai has been always used for the last three hundred years by the local population to refer to this city. Now it has become official. Many locals still call it Madras. Even though Government tried they could not legally force institutions like Madras University to change their names since these were established under a charter of the government.

We pass by Anna University, and I think of my sister (Anna is her name). I'm surprised, but I guess I should not be, that in India they drive like in the U.K., with the steering wheel on the right side, and passing also on the right. Just different to watch and manage for somebody who grew up in Italy and lives in the US like me.

We drive by a Gandhi statue, for an institution and memorial dedicated to the Mahatma. I know Gandhi was originally from the north, in fact northwest. And I've read there is some competition and animosity between north and south. But my guide states that the vast majority of people in India adore Gandhi.

License plates here start with TN, for Tamil Nadu, the South-East state we are in. Pedestrians are crossing this highway slowly, with no fear, no hurry, despite the chaotic traffic. I see five persons on one motorcycle: from front to back, a 5 year old son, then the dad, then a 7 year old or so daughter, then an infant in his mother's arms.

Cricket fields go by us. In my whole stay here in India, I'll see only one soccer field. This is still one nation where the beautiful game has not really taken hold yet. We see water trucks. My guide states there is significant water scarcity in India. Water is precious. They must have collected some from the rain last night, and are probably distributing it directly to people in the poorer districts of Chennai.

We arrive at The Leela Palace, the hotel I'm staying at, and where the conference is at. There is quite a bit of security greeting us. This is supposedly the best hotel in Chennai. About six women are waiting to greet me - I take a photo! - with their wide smiles and bright saris. There are columns and a large pool at the magnificent entrance, as well as a body scanner and baggage check.

I thank them profusely, their happy faces are contagious. I learn that Vanakam is a common friendly way to greet people in

Tamil. Two of the women escort me all the way to my room, and a couple of staff people from the hotel fight over which one takes my carry-on and my bag. What service!

The hotel lobby is elegant, modern, full of brightly colored flowers, of expensive-looking Indian sculptures and paintings, of friendly staff. They walk me into a beautiful suite!! I have a magnificent view of the bay and the Bengal Sea in the huge window of my suite. Wow!! There are food and flowers everywhere.

In fact, after a few minutes another guy arrives while I'm on the toilet with lots more goods. I notice the toilet has a hose to 'shower' private parts. I'll learn this is typical for middle and upper class Indian toilets.

I shower – incredibly forceful huge jet in the glassed shower - and shave, and feel wonderful. Rejuvenated. My feet are a bit swollen, but I feel new otherwise. And I look the part with white shirt, red tie, blue jacket, and grey pants. I'm new!

Gita Arjun greets me downstairs, at the PROGRESS Congress. She is the ob-gyn specialist who has been organizing this major national conference for years, since 1993. She spells prOGress as an acronym for Practical ObGyn Congress, which I find clever.

Before the main hall where the conference talks are being given, there is a large reception area with many sponsoring health companies displaying their innovations and products, as it's common at these types of conferences. What's different is that there are also jewelry stands, and other non-medicine related stores. I'm always glad to see a varied world, not yet completely uniformed.

I've arrived just at the end of the first session. Then there is a break, and after the session where I'm now supposed to talk. Good timing. Gita is pleasant, friendly, smiley. She introduces me to many congress participants, and some more introduce themselves. I take a bunch of pictures with them.

A nice 30ish year old Indian guy starts following me everywhere, giving me coffee - both Indian with milk, as well as black coffee -, cookies and other food. I'm treated like royalty. I do drink a couple of large cups of coffee, to beat the jet lag.

During the break, we go downstairs to an elegant and huge other hall, where the over 600 participants are having also water, drinks, coffee, snacks, and chat lively. I meet lots of other Indian colleagues. Over 95% are women, and I'd say over 80% are wearing elegant, bright, beautiful traditional Indian sari dresses. I realize I could be from the north as I'm slightly lighter skinned that people from south India.

Gita Arjun introduces me as an international star of maternal-fetal medicine and high-risk obstetrics. I'm always taken aback by such fame. We are so far from where I grew up, and even more from where I've worked the last few decades.

I feel like I'm having an out-of-body experience when they talk about me in such positive terms, I'm not sure I believe what I hear, that they are really talking about me. Everybody wants to take a picture with me in it.

I start my part at the congress by talking about SMFM, the Society for Maternal-Fetal Medicine, for which I have been President recently, and that I'm representing and publicizing here. Many in India want to become members of our society, and I'm here to offer $15 memberships!! That is a huge bargain, as I pay $450 for my regular membership…

My first lecture (labeled 'The PROGRESS Oration') is on the short cervix (the lower part of the womb), and how monitoring the cervix helps prevent preterm birth. India actually has by far the most preterm births in the world. They are #1 in this not desirable list. Having over 26 million births per year, of which over 10% before 37 weeks, they have an estimated 3 million preterm babies born every year.

I try to make my lecture interactive, and ask for audience participation. I'm so impressed how medicine is somewhat similar now around the world. I'm not even in Delhi or Mumbai, but even here in Chennai they use cervical length screening, they prescribe progesterone for a short cervix, by the same vaginal route and the same dosage.

One of the other main interventions to prevent a preterm birth, and save a baby from being born too soon, is the placement of a cerclage during pregnancy Cerclage is a stitch around the cervix to keep it closed. I emphasize the fact that cerclage was invented in India, by Dr. V. N. Shirodkar!

He first described this new technique in 1955. He published the first cases in 1957. In 1963, Dr. Shirodkar traveled to NYC to perform the procedure at the New York Hospital of Special Surgery; the procedure was successful, and the baby lived to adulthood.

In fact I get several questions on cerclage, and on its technical aspects. I'm delighted everyone speaks English, and is so intensely attentive to what we are talking about. The questions are great, and, as usual, I learn a bit myself, too, from the academic interactions.

Over 90% of ObGyns in India are women, as is my audience. In fact the percentage today of the over 600 attendees must be 98% women, as I see only a few men around. The women I meet during this congress are emancipated, smart, with no limits to their dreams and careers.

The two lectures after mine regard first twins, then preeclampsia of early onset. Again, I realize the management is not that dissimilar between Chennai and Philadelphia. Most of the quoted studies I'm familiar with, as they are from US medical journals. I learn that the biggest Indian journal of our specialty, J Obs Gyn India, is not on PubMed. That means it really does not count much.

I always learn something by listening from anyone. I write down during one of these two lectures a nice quote, by Maxwell: "If you keep on doing what you've always done, you'll keep on getting what you always gotten." So true.

My second lecture (labeled 'Keynote Address') is on how to perform a cesarean delivery. There are an estimated over 25 million cesareans done in the world every year. India has an estimated over 15% cesarean rate, quickly increasing, especially in private institutions. That means that approximately 4 million cesareans are done annually in India, an astronomical number.

China has 18 million births, with a 35% estimated cesarean delivery rate, and so is the only country that has more cesareans than India. No matter how you look at it, cesarean section is by far now the most common major operation in the world, and should be done according to evidence based principles. Once again, the audience interaction is great, with lots and lots of questions.

The lunch has excellent food. I love Indian food. For the first time in my life, I'm now tasting the real thing. I stay away, as instructed back in the US, from anything not cooked. But 90% of the buffet choices are cooked, so I dive in, and have a couple of huge servings of real, warm, delicious Indian food.

At the table, Gita's husband tells me about the state we are in, Tamil Neru, and about Tamil pride.

After lunch, I stay to listen to Gita's lecture. Gita is great. Smart and evidence-based. Well spoken. I'm impressed by her lecture, and may be even more by her, as she clearly masters the topic – disclosing medical errors – and is very clear in her exposure.

But I'm hitching to go around and visit Chennai. After her lecture, Asha and I sneak out and plan to go touring a bit later. I take a small break in my luxurious hotel room. I talk with Paola. A cleaning person comes in to clean the linens, which get changed I guess twice a day. I'm feeling fine, no jet lag with all the coffee in me.

I go on tour with Asha and two young women. We have a quiet driver who takes us everywhere in the air-conditioned Mercedes. I feel like a king. Asha is a wealth of non-stop information all day long.

She tells me that the national obstetrics and gynecology meeting in India is very political. About 7,000 colleagues go to the meeting, but no one attends the lectures, which are of poor quality, usually given by friends of the powerful organizers of the meeting.

The hotel room charges are 10 times higher from the congress organizers than from the hotel. The national congress is called AICOG, which stands for All India Congress of Obstetrics and Gynecology. This is organized by FOGSI, the Federation of Obstetric & Gynecological Societies of India.

As Asha talks about ob-gyn politics, she also points to St. George's Church. The cathedral was built in 1815. St. George's occupies an important place in the history of Christianity in India, as the Church of South India was inaugurated here on September 27, 1947. It marked the breaking down of ecclesiastical barriers between Protestants of various traditions.

There are approximately 34,000 ob-gyn members of FOGSI, divided in an incredible over 220 small little societies from all over India. It looks like anyone can have her/his own society of friends. State-level societies are also strong. But there are many more ob-gyns throughout India who are unregistered. If there are over 55,000 ob-gyns in the USA for less than 4 million births, I estimate there must be well over 100,000 India ob-gyns for their 26 million births. At least!

We arrive in an unasphalted, small square, with a beautiful temple dominating it. I hear music coming from the market stores, and I'm told about Shivaranjani. This is a musical god, and Shivaranjani is also a musical scale used in Indian classical music. I have all the love to attract god towards me: musical god.

With the two sisters, one thin beautiful and more serious, the other rounder and more smiley, as well as Asha, we walk first into an indoor market, with many many stores. We enter one, which has millions of Hindu god statues, framed pictures, and other ornaments.

In the next couple of hours, I get immersed in Hindu gods and Hindu religious myths. Ganesh is perhaps Asha's favorite god.

Also called Ganesha, Ganapati, Vinayaka and Binayak, Ganesh is one of the best-known and most worshiped deities in the Hindu pantheon.

Ganesha's elephant head makes him easy to identify. Ganesha is widely revered as the remover of obstacles, the patron of arts and sciences and the deva of intellect and wisdom. As the god of beginnings, he is honored at the start of rites and ceremonies.

Ganesha is also invoked as patron of letters and learning during writing sessions. There are many myths about his origin and birth, with the most accepted as him being the son of Shiva and Parvati. Shiva is the Supreme Being for Shaivism, one of the major traditions of modern Hinduism.

Interestingly, while Hinduism is one of the world's oldest religions, the term itself only came into common usage in the 18th century, as a European catchall word for the myriad interconnected traditions of India.

While there are millions of Hindu deities, I eventually figure out that Braham is the god of gods, so to speak, the father of all gods. That Shiva and Vishnu are also pan-Indian supreme deities. And that Ganesh is pretty popular, too.

Asha says that Ganesh, as the remover of obstacles, should be placed at the entrance of the house, to protect it from bad happenings. Ganesh has big ears to listen a lot, and a small mouth, as speaking should be much less than listening. I love Ganesh. I buy five small statues of Ganesh, to protect the houses of my parents, my sister, my brother, my in-laws, and my brother-in-law.

The shop has five stories, and we visit each one. I speak a bunch with one of the sisters who is accompanying us, who tells me that a lot of people smoke in India, tobacco but also a lot of pot. The estimates are for a 30% incidence of smoking, with almost 900,000 Indians dying from smoking consequences annually.

In India, common terms for cannabis preparations include charas (resin), ganja (flower), and bhang (seeds and leaves), with a milkshake made from bhang being one of the most common licit usages of marijuana in India.

We look at hundreds of different statues of gods. Sun is the god of gods. Fire is the highest representation. One god is of infinite power. We are all raised of the same sun. As creations of the creator. So we are all creators and gods.

That is why we bow here in India saluting others. It's called Namaste, from Sanskrit. It means, I bow to the god in you. Namaste is usually spoken with a slight bow and hands pressed together, palms touching and fingers pointing upwards, thumbs close to the chest.

The greeting may also be spoken without the gesture or the gesture performed wordlessly, carrying the same meaning. I love that: I bow to the god in you. There is such great respect for others in Hindu religion.

A phrase is often repeated in some of the walls around us in the shop. 'Tamaso Maa Jyotirgamaya' means 'From darkness, lead me to light'. It is from the Shanthi Mantra from The Bṛhadāraṇyaka Upanishad which is one of the older, primary mukhya Upanishads. The song which includes this phrase also has,

'From ignorance, lead me to truth;

From darkness, lead me to light;

From death, lead me to immortality

Aum peace, peace, peace'.

On sale there are also water cups, so you can spray water and remove all obstacles. One sister points to me Natarajan, the god of dancers. There is also Krishna, the lover boy. Everybody loves this god. The statuette that depicts it means like, 'You are giving birth to a god', and is given at baby showers.

I get educated in Shloka, which means 'song', from the root sru, 'hear'. This is a category of verse line developed from the Vedic Anustubh poetic meter. It is the basis for Indian epic verse, and may be considered the Indian verse form par excellence, occurring, as it does, far more frequently than any other meter in classical Sanskrit poetry.

The Mahabharata and Ramayana, for example, epic Indian narrative books, are written almost exclusively in shlokas. The traditional view is that this form of verse was involuntarily composed by Valmiki, the author of the Ramayana, in grief, on seeing a hunter shoot down one of two birds in love. So shlokas are mantras chanted for the gods.

We eventually exit the store, and market, and head to the temple which dominates this square. This is called Kapaleeshwarar temple. Kapaleeshwarar Temple is a temple of Shiva. The form of Shiva's consort Parvati (remember, these two conceived together Ganesh, the elephant god) worshipped at this temple is called Karpagambal, Goddess of the Wish-Yielding Tree. The temple was built around the 7th century CE in Dravidian architecture.

It's important to understand this concept of Dravidian. It is commonly brought in the conversations during my stay in Tamil Neru. The Tamils consider themselves the standard bearers of Dravidian civilization. The Dravidian civilization is the pre-Aryan civilization in India.

Dravidians are defined as speakers of the Dravidian languages, the four most important of which are all rooted in South India, such as Tamil, Malayalam (Kerala), Telugu (Telangana and Andhra Pradesh) and Kannada (Karnataka).

South Indian cultures and history are distinct from Aryan North India, and Tamil's ability to trace their identity back in an unbroken line to classical antiquity is a source of considerable pride. Since before independence in 1947, Tamil politicians have railed against caste, which they see as favoring light-skinned Brahmins, and against the Hindi language, seen as North Indian cultural imperialism.

As an example of Tamil pride, during the conflict in nearby Sri Lanka, many Indian Tamil politicians loudly defended the Tamil Tigers, the organization that assassinated Rajiv Gandhi in a village near Chennai in 1991.

The Tamil Tigers were a Tamil militant organization based in northeastern Sri Lanka. Founded in May 1976 by Velupillai

Prabhakaran, it waged a secessionist nationalist insurgency to create an independent state of Tamil Eelam in the north and east of Sri Lanka for Tamil people.

This campaign led to the Sri Lankan Civil War, which ran from 1983 until 2009, when the Tamil Tigers were eventually defeated, with the financial and strategic help of China, by the Sri Lankan Armed Forces during the presidency of Mahinda Rajapaksa.

Let's go back and speak about this temple, Chennai's most active and impressive. According to the Puranas (Hindu religious texts), Shakti (the god of strength) worshipped Shiva in the form of a peacock, giving the vernacular name Mylai to the area that developed around the temple - mayil is Tamil for 'peacock'. Shiva is worshiped as Kapaleeswarar, and is represented by the lingam.

The lingam is an abstract or aniconic representation of the Hindu deity Shiva, usually in phallic shape, as a symbol of the energy and potential of Shiva himself. The lingam is often represented as resting on yoni - Sanskrit word, literally 'vulva', 'origin' or 'source'.

Shiva's consort, Parvati, is depicted as Karpagambal. Goddess Karpagambal, due to a curse, became a pea-hen and did penance here to get back her original personality. The presiding deity is revered in the 7th century Tamil Saiva canonical work, the Tevaram, written by Tamil saint poets known as the nayanars, and classified as Paadal Petra Sthalam.

The temple has numerous shrines, with those of Kapaleeswarar and Karpagambal being the most prominent. The temple complex houses many halls.

The temple's name is derived from the words kapalam (head) and eeshwarar, an alias of lord Shiva. According to the Puranas, during the meeting of Brahma and Shiva at top of Mount Kailash, Brahma failed to show the due respect to Shiva. Consequently, Shiva plucked of one of Brahma's heads (kapalams). In an act of penance, Brahma came down to the site of Mylapore and installed a lingam to please Shiva.

We should expand now briefly a bit more about Hinduism's deities. Hinduism has been called the religion of 330 million deities, which is a deliberate exaggeration but gives a sense of the myriads of gods that exists in this fascinating religion.

Some Hindus believe that the various incarnations of these deities, called avatars, all derive from one central divine being known as Brahman. Others believe that Brahman manifests as three centrally powerful gods, Brahma, Vishnu and Shiva. These three are known as Trimurti. Other Hindus believe that each deity is distinct and should be worshipped separately.

An example of how one can quickly get lost among the many names of Indian gods is the fact that Vishnu alone is considered to have 11 avatars, or manifestations. These are Matsya, a fish; Kurma, a turtle; Varaha, a boar; Narasimha, a lion; Vamana, a dwarf; Parasurama, a man wielding an axe; Rama, the hero of the Ramayana; Balarama, an earlier incarnation of Krishna; Krishna, a well-loved god who appears in many stories; the Buddha; and Kalki, the horseman who will usher in the Kali Yuga, the age of destruction. You see, one deity, and I'm already lost!

Vedas (large body of Indian knowledge texts) deities include Agni, the god of fire, Indra, the god of thunder and war, Brahma and Surya, the sun god. These personify elements of the natural world.

Many myths have been said to occur here at Kapaleeshwarar temple. Shiva's son Murugan received the spear (Sakthi Vel) for the destruction of a demon from Parvati here. Brahma had worshipped here to get rid of his ego and get back his power to create.

The four Vedas have worshipped here. Sukracharya worshipped the Lord here and got back his lost eye. Rama has worshipped here and won the war against Ravana and brought back Sita from Lanka. The daughter of Sivanesa Chettiar Angam Poompavai lost her life due to a snake bite and was later resurrected here by the powers of Thirugnana Sambandar.

The commonly held view is that the temple was built in the 7th century CE by the ruling Pallavas. This view is based on references to the temple in the hymns of the Nayanmars (which, however, place it by a sea shore). Thirugnanasambandar's 6th song in Poompavaipathikam and Arunagirinathar's 697th song in Thirumylai Thirupugazh, make clear reference to the Kapaleeswarar temple being located on the seashore in Mylapore.

The scholarly view that accounts for the discrepancies is that the original temple was built on the shore but was destroyed by the Portuguese and the current masonry temple (which is 1-1.5 km from the shore) was built by the Vijayanagar kings during the 16th century, using some remains of the old temple. The temple is maintained and administered by the Hindu Religious and Endowment Board of the Government of Tamil Nadu.

There are inscriptions dating back to 12th century inside the temple. The temple's stunning and iconic 120-feet gopuram (gateway tower) was built during 1906 with brightly rainbow-colored stucco figures adorning it.

The Kapaleeshwarar temple is of typical Dravidian architectural style, with the gopuram overpowering the street on which the temple sits. This temple is also a testimonial for the vishwakarmas sthapathis. There are two entrances to the temple marked by the gopuram on either side. The eastern gopuram is about 40 meter high, while the smaller western gopuram faces the sacred tank.

The vahanas (Sanskrit for 'vehicles') at the temple include the bull, Adhikaranandi, elephant, bandicoot, peacock, goat and parrot, while a golden chariot is a recent addition. Statues of the god and the goddess are seated on a vahana or chariot which is brought in a procession around the temple while the temple band plays music.

Devotees traditionally gather around the vahanas and consider it a privilege to pull / lift the God and the Goddess on the vahana. There is also a peacock and a peahen caged inside the temple, to symbolize the tradition that Karpagambal had come in the form of peahen to plead to Kapaleeshwarar.

The temple priests perform the pooja (rituals) during festivals and on a daily basis. Like other Shiva temples of Tamil Nadu, the priests belong to the Shaivaite community, a Brahmin sub-caste. Each ritual comprises four steps: abhisheka (sacred bath), alangaram (decoration), neivethanam (food offering) and deepa aradanai (waving of lamps) for both Kapaleeswarar and Karpagambal.

The worship is held amidst music with nagaswaram (pipe instrument) and tavil (percussion instrument), religious instructions in the Vedas (sacred text) read by priests and prostration by worshippers in front of the temple mast.

On the side of the entrance, we take our shoes off and give them to a nice Indian in special shop who will keep them for us. We walk from now on barefooted, and I do feel Indian now, like I'm all immersed in the culture and the place.

The two sisters tell me that each one of the hundreds of statues making up the brilliantly-colored tall tower (gopuram) at the entrance is hand-made and painted. Under the monumental entrance, one is supposed to completely lie down on the floor, belly down, one arm extended forward, in worship.

They idea is that 'I kiss the land you (the deity, which is all of us) walk on'. One is supposed to touch the ground with chest and forehand, as well as abdomen and legs. I love the powerfulness of the gesture and its deep meaning.

They explain to me another marvelous Hindu belief. Each of us is supposed to have a third eye. This eye is not supposed to look in front of us, or around us, but inside us. It's the most important eye, the eye of introspection.

Inside us is god, so the third eye also looks at the deity in our inner self. If we concentrate enough, by meditation, on using this third eye effectively, nothing outside of our body should matter anymore. We are supposed to learn to look inside, like in deep meditation, at the divinity in ourselves. This third eye is also the eye of knowledge.

Shiva, again one of the principal deities in Hinduism, is the god of killing ignorance. Shiva means auspiciousness. Auspicious refers to something that promises success; is propitious, favorable, and used for example as 'an auspicious occasion'.

There are a few people in the temple, it's not so crowed as during festivals and other religious occasions. Some are praying, and chanting softly in Sanskrit.

I'm told about other Hindu beliefs. These are wonderful stories about how to relate to others, how to be altruistic, friendly, and always see the best in others. An example is the meaning of a coconut. The coconut is rough outside, but pure and good inside. The similitude is regarding people. One should not judge from the outside. Inside people are good, even if they may not seem so from the outside. I'll never look at a coconut the same way.

As we enter the temple, we put tilaka on our foreheads. The tilaka (at times also spelled tilak, or thilak) is a mark created by the application of powder or paste on the forehead. There are several different types, according to different Indian regions and traditions.

As examples, Shaktas, worshippers of the various forms of the Goddess (Devi), wear a large red dot of kumkum (vermillion or red turmeric) on the forehead. The Vaishnava tilaka instead consists of a long vertical marking starting from just below the hairline to almost the end of one's nose tip, and they are also known as Urdhva Pundra. It is intercepted in the middle by an elongated U. There may be two marks on the temples as well. This tilaka is traditionally made with sandalwood paste.

The other major tilaka variant is often worn by the followers of Shiva, known by the names of Rudra-tilaka and Tripundra. It consists of three horizontal bands across the forehead with a single vertical band or circle in the middle. This is traditionally done with sacred ash from fire sacrifices. This variant is the more ancient of the two and shares many common aspects with similar markings worn across the world.

But far more common here seem to be the dot-shaped tilaka. The sisters draw a red Kumkuma tilaka on my head. I'll read later that marking someone's forehead with a fragrant paste, such as of sandalwood or vermilion, is a welcome and expression of honor when a guest arrives.

There are many other powders available to make tilaka here. Vibhooti (or Vibhuti) is a white sacred ash which is made of burnt dried wood in Agamic rituals. Hindu devotees apply vibhuti traditionally as three horizontal lines across the forehead and other parts of the body to honor Shiva. The sisters put some white vibhuti on top of the red kumkuma on my forehad, to honor me I guess even more.

They explain that Bindi is a black tilak worn on the middle of the low forehead, between the eyebrows, by Hindu married women. This distinguishes them by others. Makeup or jewelry can also be work instead of the Bindi, always in black.

Red and white colors for tilak are auspicious. White is there to remind us that we are nothing but ash. Red is usually the color of gods; so the sisters are putting it on me because I'm a god. Red is also like a rosary, signifying the passion.

Women are expected to wear a tilak, especially if married. Black tilak are also sometimes worn by women if widowed.

But the three women with me, now all with they foreheads covered in tilak powders, say in modern India now tilaks are worn often just for fashion. Often the color has nothing to do with Hindu religious meanings, but is chosen just to match to one's clothes.

I realize now reliving this Indian trip, that Indian women love colors, and India is a very colorful place. I guess all these reds, oranges, yellows, greens, look great on Indian women given their dark skin and black hair.

Men instead wear the tilak only if they are going to temple. I now have a nice round large red tilak between my bushy black eyebrows.

The signs inside the temple are in Tamil, which is written in characters which are impossible for me to discern, a mix of Greek

Cyrillic Arabic or whatever other language has written characters different than European languages.

Asha shows me a wonderful, colorful display of figurines and small swings hanging from a tree. Like a Christmas tree with lots of ornaments. She tells me here couples who have trouble getting pregnant come and hang some of these figures.

Some are bright yellow, wooden squares with fences, hanging like swings, containing a small blue baby, for wishing to have a baby. There are also messages on paper left on the tree, sometimes wrapped inside pieces of cloth. They are wishes to the gods.

Indians can tell from how they are organized what they probably say inside. Some are wishes to get married. Some to get a house. All the three women with me have no doubt that whatever wishes are put here on this tree, in this Kapaleeshwarara Temple, will for sure come true. All around us, the temple is covered with donations to the gods.

Once out of the temple, we get our shoes back. Near the place where our shoes are, there is a lady that is quintessential India. I sneak a photo. She must be over 70 years old, grayish hair but still with some recalcitrant Indian black in them, probably less than 5 feet tall, a colorful orange green red sari, with her belly with a pannus hanging out over her skirt, a nice red bow in the hair, and barefoot. From the look of her feet, I wonder if she ever wore shoes. I love it.

We walk around Chennai a bit. Asha does know this city some, and the sisters, being from here, know it even better. Nearby the temple, there is a large body of water, a tank, man-made, and gated all around now. It is about the size of ten Olympic swimming pools.

My guides tell me that this tank indeed belongs to temple, and is used for people to wash their bodies. They tell me that Chennai completely flooded in 2015. This pool completely overflooded. The 2015 South Indian floods resulted from heavy rainfall generated by the annual northeast monsoon in November–December 2015.

They affected the Coromandel Coast region of the South Indian states of Tamil Nadu and Andhra Pradesh, and the union territory of Puducherry, with Tamil Nadu and the city of Chennai particularly hard-hit. More than 500 people were killed and over 1.8 million people were displaced. The estimates of damages and losses ranged from nearly $3 billion to over $16 billion.

We walk alongside the body of water, in a street were scooters and cars come shooting at us at blazing speed even if it looks like this should be just an unasphalted walking path.

There is a farmer market at the end of the huge pool. All kinds of vegetables and fruits are on display, most of very bright colors. I can only tell what about 50% of them are. Many must be typical of India, and perhaps just South India.

They tell me about Jallikattu, a traditional spectacle in which a bull is released into a crowd of people, and multiple human participants attempt to grab the large hump on the bull's back with both arms and hang on to it while the bull attempts to escape.

Participants hold the hump for as long as possible, attempting to bring the bull to a stop. In some cases, participants must ride long enough to remove flags on the bull's horns. Jallikattu is typically practiced here in the Indian state of Tamil Nadu as a part of Pongal celebrations on Mattu Pongal day, which occurs annually in January.

The sisters say that now this game has been banned in Chennai, but I know the controversy in the state of Tamil Nadu continues.

My guides also make me laugh. They say it's usually very hot in Chennai, and today is no exception. They say that people become usually anuric (this is a medical term meaning 'not making any urine') since it's so hot. "That is why there are no public toilets here, they are not needed!"

According to Hinduism, death is not the end all. The soul after death enters another body. So really everybody dies, but

44

nobody dies. The soul is the pure part of us. We can be reborn several million times. We can be reborn as humans again, or also as an animal of any type, or anything else.

The worse you were in the prior life, the lower entity you will become in the next life. One is reborn as human if she did something good in last life. Nirvana is when you become one with the divine power - it happens if you were inner-looking in last life with no attachment to earthy things and your third eye was working a lot. Nirvana is when you are released.

Politics permeates India. I notice the ubiquitous round smiley face of one woman in so many posters around Chennai and this state of Tamil Nadu. I'm told her name is J. Jayalalithaa, and she has been in the recent past the Chief Minister of Tamil Nadu five times, from 1991 until 2016.

Jayaram Jayalalithaa (born Komalavalli, February 24th, 1948 – December 5th, 2016) was an Indian actress turned politician. From 1989 she was the general secretary of the All India Anna Dravida Munnetra Kazhagam (AIADMK), a Dravidian party whose cadre revered her as their Amma (mother), Puratchi Thalaivi (revolutionary leader) and Thanga Tharagai (golden maiden).

In fact, we also see the huge memorial for her, where she is called Puratchi Thialaivar, revolutionary leader. On top of this large, over 40 feet tall structure, there is a golden winged horse, over a massive pedestal.

Her critics in the media and the opposition accused her of fostering a personality cult, and of demanding absolute loyalty from AIADMK legislators and ministers who often publicly prostrated themselves before her.

Jayalalithaa first came into prominence as a leading film actress in the mid-1960s. Though she had entered the profession reluctantly, upon the urging of her mother to support the family, Jayalalithaa worked prolifically. She appeared in 140 films between 1961 and 1980, primarily in the Tamil, Telugu and Kannada languages.

Jayalalithaa received praise for her versatility as an actress and for her dancing skills, earning the sobriquet 'queen of Tamil cinema'. Among her frequent co-stars was M. G. Ramachandran, or MGR, a Tamil cultural icon who leveraged his immense popularity with the masses into a successful political career.

In 1982, when MGR was chief minister, Jayalalithaa joined the AIADMK, the party he founded. Her political rise was rapid; within a few years she became AIADMK propaganda secretary and was elected to the Rajya Sabha, the upper house of India's Parliament.

After MGR's death in 1987, Jayalalithaa proclaimed herself his political heir and, having fought off the faction headed by Janaki Ramachandran, MGR's widow, emerged as the sole leader of the AIADMK. Following the 1989 election, she became Leader of the Opposition to the DMK-led government headed by Karunanidhi, her adversary.

In 1991 Jayalalithaa became chief minister, Tamil Nadu's youngest, for the first time. She earned a reputation for a punishing work ethic and for centralizing state power among a coterie of bureaucrats; her council of ministers, whom she often shuffled around, were largely ceremonial in nature.

The successful cradle-baby scheme, which enabled mothers to anonymously offer their newborns for adoption, emerged during this time. Despite an official salary of only a rupee a month, Jayalalithaa indulged in public displays of wealth, culminating in a lavish wedding for her foster son in 1995.

In the 1996 election, the AIADMK was nearly wiped out at the hustings; Jayalalithaa herself lost her seat. The new Karunanidhi government filed several corruption cases against her, and she had to spend time in jail. Her fortunes revived in the 1998 general election, as the AIADMK became a key component of Prime Minister Atal Bihari Vajpayee's 1998–99 government; her withdrawal of support toppled it and triggered another general election just a year later.

The AIADMK returned to power in 2001, although Jayalalithaa was personally disbarred from contesting due to the corruption cases. Within a few months of her taking oath as chief minister, in September 2001, she was disqualified from holding office, and forced to cede the chair to loyalist O. Panneerselvam.

Upon her acquittal six months later, Jayalalithaa returned as chief minister to complete her term. Noted for its ruthlessness to political opponents, many of whom were arrested in midnight raids, her government grew unpopular.

Another period (2006-2011) in the opposition followed, before Jayalalithaa was sworn in as chief minister for the fourth time after the AIADMK swept the 2011 assembly election. Her government received attention for its extensive social-welfare agenda, which included several subsidized 'Amma'-branded goods such as canteens, bottled water, salt, cement, medicine shops and so on.

Three years into her tenure, she was convicted in a disproportionate-assets case, rendering her disqualified to hold office. She returned as chief minister after being acquitted in May 11, 2015. In the 2016 assembly election, she was voted back into office. That September 22nd, she fell severely ill and, following 75 days of hospitalization, died on December 5th, 2016 due to cardiac arrest.

She was so loved that many people committed suicide. My friends say that her second in command killed Jayalalithaa by slow poisoning. Her death was not announced for 25 hours, as authorities were so afraid of the chaos it would have generated.

We see along our route the statue of Gandhi in Marina Beach Road. We drive by the University of Madras. University of Madras is the alma mater of two Indian Physics Nobel Laureates, including Subrahmanyan Chandrasekhar, five Presidents of India, including A.P.J. Abdul Kalam, and several notable mathematicians including Srinivasa Ramanujan.

While most buildings here are so Indian, some are definitively colonial. The tower at Madras University is a bit of both, colonial in its elegance and large size, Indian in its half-globe-shaped large multiple cream colored roofs tops, and red walls.

As we drive more along the road which coasts the ocean, they tell me about Swami Vivekanada, who was the sage who brought yoga to US. Swami Vivekanada demonstrated yoga postures at a World Fair in Chicago in the 1890s. This generated much interest and laid the grounds for the welcoming of many other Yogis and Swamis from India in the years that followed.

My hosts tell me that there are no guards on the beach. So if you swim and drown, nobody notices. The water is warm, but it pulls you out, and can be dangerous. Today is a beautiful mostly clear day. I'm surprised not more people are in the ocean.

Still along the shore, there is a very tall, like a ten-story high, tower which is way bigger than anything around us. It is the Chennai lighthouse. The Madras Light House (just to make you laugh, I'll give you its name in Tamil too: சென்னைக் கலங்கரை விளக்கம்) is a lighthouse facing the Bay of Bengal on the East coast of the Indian Subcontinent. It is a famous landmark on the Marina Beach in Chennai, India.

It was built by the East Coast Constructions and Industries in 1976 replacing the old lighthouse in the northern direction. It also houses the meteorological department and was restricted to visitors. On November 16th, 2013, it was reopened to visitors.

It is one of the few lighthouses in the world with an elevator. It is also the only lighthouse in India within the city limits. It is a green lighthouse, with a solar panel for power.

Its history is important, as there has been a lighthouse here for a much longer time. By the end of the 18th century, the Madras Presidency encompassed much of south India and also Ceylon (Sri Lanka). As its capital, the city of Madras served as the nerve center of the sea trade controlled by the British East India Company.

Ships approaching the shore of Madras after nightfall faced the risk of running aground on the shoals of Covelong (Kovalam) in the south and the sand-banks of Armagon and Pulicat in the north. So the lighthouse in a sense reminds us all of why Chennai, the former Madras, came to be such an important city, the biggest and most important city in South India, and the 4th largest in all the subcontinent.

There are many poor fish stands along the shore side of the road. Each has many different kinds of fish in display, under the sun, in the heat. The smell is pungent, but one I grew up with in my home town of Pescara, Italy, and love.

Most are manned by middle-aged Indian women, obese and with their pannus (overhanging large abdomens) sticking out of their saris. Men instead seem to be those overseeing things only. I can only image how these women will smell when they go home.

The shore, on our left as we are driving on the coastal road, is littered by rubbish, everywhere, especially near the road. I doubt anyone ever cleans it up. Some of the clutter seems old, there for a long time. There are even sheep and goats roaming on the sand. There is plenty of waste to eat for them.

There are even some huts on the sand. Mostly nothing more than tents, made of a piece of cloth over four rudimentary stands. Asha and the driver tell me people live in these shacks permanently. These are homes. Under them, many only 4 by 4 yards in size, I see 8-10 people sitting down next to each other on the sand under the canopy. I can only imagine hygiene in these incredible living conditions.

Interestingly, the word 'bungalow', which could describe some of these 'homes', comes from the word 'bangla', meaning 'Bengali-style'. We are indeed on the gulf of Bengal, with Bengal usually being referred to as the region between present-day Bangladesh and West India.

A bit everywhere, hanging on long ropes fixed on wooden poles, clothes hang in the strong sun and the light breeze to dry. Everything is in the open. This is life on a Chennai beach.

There are many shacks both on the sand along the shore on the left of the street we are driving on, as well as on the right, where they completely line the side of the road. My friends tell me these are Government houses built after the tsunami. They were given to the poor fishermen community.

The 2004 Indian Ocean earthquake occurred at 00:58:53 UTC on December 26th, with the epicenter off the west coast of Sumatra, Indonesia. The shock had a moment magnitude of 9.1–9.3 and a maximum Mercalli intensity of IX (Violent). It was the third-largest earthquake ever recorded on a seismograph and had the longest duration of faulting ever observed, between 8.3 and 10 minutes.

The undersea megathrust earthquake was caused when the Indian Plate was subducted by the Burma Plate and triggered a series of devastating tsunamis along the coasts of most landmasses bordering the Indian Ocean. It eventually killed 230,000–280,000 people in 14 countries, inundating coastal communities with waves up to 30 meters (100 feet) high. It was one of the deadliest natural disasters in recorded history.

The tsunami arrived in the state of Tamil Nadu along the southeast coast of the Indian mainland shortly after 9:00 a.m. Tamil Nadu was extensively damaged, as the tsunami run-up was 4–5 meters (13.1-16.4 feet) in some coastal districts.

The duration between the waves varied from about 15 minutes to about 90 minutes. The 13 km (8.1 miles) Marina Beach in Chennai, where we are traveling now, was battered by this huge tsunami which swept across the beach taking morning walkers unaware.

As we get back to the hotel, I learn more details of some wonderful Indian greetings. Bowing in respect is called Namaste. Shukriya means 'thank you' in Hindi, spoken in most of India, in particular in the north. Nandri instead is 'thank you' in Tamil. Vanakkam means 'hello' in Chennai Tamil. Of course the younger sister needs to always spell these words on my iPhone as I take notes, as it would be impossible to get the right spelling otherwise.

Back at the hotel, I take a beautiful picture from my huge window of the Chennai beach in front of me, with a placid lagoon, and tropical beautiful cured vegetation all over my view. How different things can look. I'm glad I experienced also the true, poor, messy, fishy, wild side of the Chennai shore.

I realize how tired I am. Jetlag is still with me, as I've been no-stop all day. I sleep 1.5 hours in my magnificent room. I wake up by myself spontaneously, restored, new. A shower and clean clothes complete the awakening.

We have dinner with Gita, as well as her husband, family and a few colleagues, in the lower floor of the hotel. There are about 20 invited guests, the main faculty speakers and their families, if they are accompanied by them.

The food is buffet style again, and simply delicious. I have some coconut based soup. And lots of other spicy entrees, with plenty of flavors and vegetables. There are all kinds of food, all perfectly spiced. Gulab Jamun is a sweet curd milk dessert, with plenty of sugar. Of course I taste everything, as long as it is cooked.

We talk about the Vesthi, which is the skirt worn by guys in Tamil. The dhoti, also known as panche, vesti, dhuti, mardani, chaadra, dhotar, and pancha, is a traditional men's garment worn in the Indian subcontinent. It is a rectangular piece of unstitched cloth, usually around 4.5 meters (15 feet) long, wrapped around the waist and the legs and knotted at the waist.

I'm told about the Irula people, who are snake catchers. The world 'Irular' means 'dark people', and this ethic group lives in the Nilgiri Mountains, in the states of Tamil Nadu and Kerala. Traditionally, the main occupation of the Irulas has been snake and rat catching. They also work as laborers (coolies) in the fields of the landlords during the sowing and harvesting seasons or in the rice mills. Fishing is also a major occupation.

Rats destroy a quarter of the grain grown on Tamil Nadu-area farms annually. To combat this pest, Irula men use a traditional earthen pot fumigation method. Smoke is blown through their mouths, which leads to severe respiratory and heart problems.

As an example of how their unique skill are used, Masi Sadaiyan and Vadivel Gopal from the Irula tribe of Tamil Nadu were brought in, along with two translators, earlier in 2017 to work with detection dogs to track down and capture giant snakes in Key Largo, Florida. They captured 14 pythons in less than two week.

We also discuss India's obstetrics. Amazingly, there are 26 million births per year in India. That is 20% of the world births!! In 2 years and a couple of months, India makes the population of Italy!

Interestingly, my colleagues state that 96% of the deliveries now happen in institutions, e.g. hospitals and birth centers, and not at home or in the fields like in the past. This is at least in some states, like this one of Tamil Nadu, where a law was passed which incentivizes hospital births. In fact, women and their families get paid for delivering in a safe environment with professionals present.

The state also pays the patients for the four required prenatal care visits, for the delivery, and for the neonatal vaccinations. I soak in all I'm told. I love learning so much regarding such a fascinating culture I know so little about.

Sunday July 30, 2017

I have a good but short night rest. I've loved this Leela Hotel room in Chennai. I read on the back of my room door that it's listed for 8,691 rupees, which is about the equivalent of about $135. This room would be over $300 in the US.

I have to wake up at 4:30am to catch the early plane to Coimbatore. All is quiet. It's really still the middle of the night. Nonetheless, I feel great. I had packed the night before, so I'm quickly ready after shower and shave, and meet drivers and accompanying people downstairs in the lobby. All my expenses have been paid, so my check-out takes a second.

There is no traffic in the early morning Chennai darkness. Asha still is talking and educating me. Conversation reverts to health care in India. She says private hospitals are very expensive. One can pay $50,000 for an operation. There is no culture of academic centers.

Over 80% of hospitals are private, and owned by doctors. Most are small, 100 beds or less. The doctors get to be very wealthy. And are in complete control of finances, as patients pay out of pocket. The many doctors who do not own a hospital are salaried, and the pay for these doctors is about the same as the US.

These doctors work a lot, as their employers 'own' them, as Asha says. Asha says she has been recruited back to India several times. She has always declined these opportunities. She feels like she would have to see patients all the time, without protected time to do research or teach.

At the airport, we meet a person who will be accompanying us through. There is really a huge connection of people looking over you here in India. Indians all tend to talk a lot, and are very friendly. At least this is my impression throughout the trip.

One of the most interesting and characteristic traits is the bobbling of the head as Indians talk. The head bobble, or Indian head shake, refers to a common gesture found in South Asian cultures, most notably in India. The motion usually consists of a side-to-side tilting of the head in arcs along the coronal plane.

The head bobble can mean a lot of things. It's there mostly to acknowledge understanding. Or to convey agreement with what's been said. Or to just give feedback to the talker that the person bobbling is listening attentively. A form of nonverbal communication, it can therefore mean 'Yes', 'Good', 'Ok' or 'I understand', depending on the context. I love it.

The doctor greeting us here has a nice big smile. He is very reassuring, as I am for sure out of my usual surroundings here.

The Indigo plane we board is modern. There are a lot of people on the plane, even if it's so early. We board all together, like in fact we did for the Emirates flight in Dubai. Here though pretty much all passengers are Indians, in this national flight, in fact within one state, Tamil Nadu.

Again I feel like I'm in a documentary. I'm looking in a fascinating part of the world, as I guess only a few lucky non-nationals have probably ever done.

Indian women and men seem to gain weight in middle age. Those less than 30 are usually very thin and in great shape. After that, only the poor (who are still many, but not on this plane) remain thin.

Indians also seem to have an excuse or a trick for everything. For example, Asha says her trick for authorities not to take her carry-on and check it is to say that she has medicines in it. She also refuses to give her seat away if asked, as she would say she has arthritis.

Many women wear the sari wrapping and put it on their shoulder. A sari, saree, or shari is a female garment from the Indian subcontinent that consists of a drape varying from five to nine yards (4.5 to 8 meters) in length and two to four feet (60 to 120 cm) in breadth that is typically wrapped around the waist, with one end draped over the shoulder, baring the midriff.

The sari is usually worn over a petticoat, with a fitted upper garment commonly called a blouse (ravike in South India and choli elsewhere). The blouse has short sleeves and is usually cropped at the midriff. The sari is associated with elegance and is widely regarded as a symbol of grace in cultures of the Indian subcontinent.

Asha explains that it's not that easy to wear a sari, as the garment can keep falling from the shoulder. But Indian women are very proud of their saris, and wear them happily. The silk is magnificent, and the colors usually bright and beautiful. India of course it's famous for its silk, which comes from all over the country.

We are sitting in the first row of the airplane. I notice the pilot is Sikh, as he wears a turban. Sikhs originate from North India, in Punjab. Sikh means 'disciple', or 'learner'. Sikhism is a monotheistic Indian religion that originated at the end of the 15th century. It is one of the youngest of the major world religions.

The fundamental beliefs of Sikhism, articulated in the sacred scripture Guru Granth Sahib, include faith and meditation on the name of the one creator, unity of all humankind, engaging in selfless service, striving for social justice for the benefit and prosperity of all, and honest conduct and livelihood while living a householder's life. In the early 21st century there were nearly 25 million Sikhs worldwide, the great majority of them living in the Indian state of Punjab.

Sikhism is based on the spiritual teachings of Guru Nanak, the first Guru, and the ten successive Sikh gurus. Guru Nanak established Kartarpur (Creator's town) around 1520 and gathered the original core of the Sikh Panth (community) there.

After the death of the tenth Guru, Guru Gobind Singh, the Sikh scripture, Guru Granth Sahib, became the literal embodiment of the eternal, impersonal Guru, where the scripture's word serves as the spiritual guide for Sikhs. Sikhism rejects claims that any particular religious tradition has a monopoly on Absolute Truth.

Sikhism emphasizes simran, meaning meditation on the words of the Guru Granth Sahib, that can be expressed musically through kirtan or internally through Nam Japo (repeat God's name) as a means to feel God's presence. It teaches followers to avoid the 'Five Thieves' (lust, rage, greed, attachment and conceit). Hand in hand, secular life is considered to be intertwined with the spiritual life.

Guru Nanak taught that living an 'active, creative, and practical life' of 'truthfulness, fidelity, self-control and purity' is above the metaphysical truth, and that the ideal man is one who 'establishes union with God, knows His Will, and carries out that Will'.

Sikhism is a relatively recent religion, that evolved in times of religious persecution. Two of the Sikh gurus - Guru Arjan and Guru Tegh Bahadur, after they refused to convert to Islam, were tortured and executed by the Mughal rulers. The persecution of Sikhs triggered the founding of the Khalsa, as an order to protect the freedom of conscience and religion.

Interestingly, some other Indians at the airport are wearing tunics and hats – all white – very similar to those I saw earlier this month in M'zab, the desert region in Algeria were some of my Muslim friends are from. Asha goes on to say that she thinks Indian Americans have seen a lot of violence against them in the US, and have been treated in a somewhat demeaning way.

Health remains precarious in some parts of India. There is still plenty of leprosy in Mumbai, Asha says. Regarding pregnancy, she states that there are about 65,000 pregnancy-related deaths every year in India. Considering there are less than 270,000 pregnancy-related annual deaths in the whole world, this is a big number. The rate comes out to be about 400 maternal deaths per 100,000 pregnancies, compared to less than 10 per 100,000 in many European countries.

In the large hospital in Mumbai that Asha knows, there are about 100 deliveries a day. Breech-presenting babies are delivered vaginally. The rich get planned cesarean deliveries. The poor have a very low cesarean rate.

Eventually I get some rest from the continuous teaching. I sleep like a baby during the rest of the short flight. In fact, the plane hitting the asphalt wakes me up abruptly. I think we have crashed!

The sun has come out and illuminates Coimbatore by the time we land. There is a lot of construction going on, holes in the pavement everywhere. I notice many cars are of brands unknown to me. One is called Innova, which I assume is an Indian car, but later discover is sold by Toyota here in India only.

Another car has in the back the name 'Mahindra'. I also assume this is an Indian car. I later learn that Mahindra and Mahindra Limited (M&M) is an Indian multinational car manufacturing corporation headquartered in Mumbai, Maharashtra, India. It is one of the largest vehicle manufacturers by production in India and the largest manufacturer of tractors in the world. It is a part of Mahindra Group, an Indian conglomerate.

A Mahindra KUV 100 car is waiting for us. This is lovely. It's not only the traveling by itself I like. It's the being pampered so well!! Despite the nice car we are in, I notice that even the driver is bare footed, like so many of the people walking around Coimbatore.

The hotel is new, less than 9 months old. Again, we are in the best hotel in town. I'll never get used to this, even if it happens routinely for me now while I travel around the world to give lectures in obstetrics and maternal-fetal medicine.

I enjoy breakfast, and a nice coffee, more American (diluted, large cup) than Italian (espresso), with a nice touch of milk. I take a photo with Gopi, who has the nicest smile and the most noticeable head-bobbing in the group. His English has such a wonderful Indian accent, I love it.

Gopi is the nickname of Dr. P.M. Gopinath, the Director for the Institute of Obstetrics and Gynecology & IVF in Chennai. As we drive back to the hotel with Asha and Gopi, both of them keep on educating me about India.

On the car ride over to the place where the conference is, Asha tells me she has been to Coimbatore innumerous times, and knows the city well. Coffee and tea are grown in this region. We see again many billboards with the face of Jayalalithaa, the former head of this state, Tamil Nadu.

Asha says she was like Robin Hood. She took from the rich, and gave to the poor. She was very intelligent. She passed away in December 2016. The entire Chennai, the capital of the state, shut down.

We arrive at the Womens Center of Coimbatore, where I'll give my next two talks. At the entrance, we are greeted by the Director of the Womens Center, Mirudhubashini Govindarajan (who I'll refer to as Mirudhu from now on, as all call her), and her husband, Mister G (as everyone calls him).

Mirudhu is wearing, as she always will during these two days in Coimbatore, an elegant sari. She is very tall, has a commanding but caring presence, and a wonderful, reassuring, friendly smile. Mister G is also very affable, perhaps more gentle as he does not carry the 'Director' role.

He seems to be a 'Mister Thatcher', as Margaret Thatcher's (former Prime Minister in the UK) husband was famously called. Mirudhu and Mister G seem to form a marvelous pair. She is more the clinician and symbol, he is more the business manager. I'll meet later their son, who seems to also be of major help with the family business, by being the site manager.

All here in India seems to be about personal relations. While I'm afraid the people attending the conference, supposedly starting at 10:10am, are waiting, Mirudhu welcomes Asha and I in her office, clearly the CEO office, where she has a commanding chair and table. Everything and everyone revolve around her.

We go through at least 30 minutes of pleasantries, where we hear about their private hospital, how they built it from nothing, and clearly how proud they are of the good clinical care they provide. Mirudhu and Mister G seem to be truly good people.

They explain to me this is very much a local conference. In fact, most of the audience is made up of staff - doctors nurses and others - who work at the Womens Center, or at other nearby obstetric facilities they collaborate with. Mirudhu apologies several times for the fact that there'll be a small crowd. I reassure her, sincerely, that I adore small crowds, with whom I can have closer interactions.

We are joined by a couple of other speakers, who also came from outside Coimbatore, in their case from other parts of India. The respect of everyone, and in particular Asha, for Mirudhu, is palpable. She eventually tells us, with no rush, we can move towards the conference room.

To my surprise, there are actually almost 100 people waiting for us in the conference room of the Womens Center. That is more than I expected actually. I'm told to seat in one of the four seats upfront, with Asha, Mirudhu, and another main speaker.

There is only one man in audience. The rest are women, mostly I would say in their thirties, almost all wearing beautiful colorful saris. I'm introduced by Mirudhu as an international star, and given the first most important lecture spot.

I have a nice blue jacket, with golden buttons, a blue with big large poke dots tie, dark grey pants, a white shirt, and I am tanned. The pictures of me talking with a microphone in my hand come out nice.

After the first lecture, I answer at least ten questions, which I love to do. The women in the audience are clearly smart, well read, and clinicians, as they have very practical insightful questions. I always learn when I teach. From one of the questions, we all come up with the need to do more studies on what kind of suture would be best for closing a cesarean section wound.

I also learn that Indian babies seem to mature more quickly, and I do not think that is unreasonable, as other races, as for example African-American, have more mature babies for the same gestational age at birth compared to, for example, white babies.

Indian babies therefore have more meconium-stained amniotic fluid before they are born, another sign of maturity. They also tend to have a larger amount of amniotic fluid, and I wonder if that's linked in any ways to higher maternal glucose, or to other factors.

Dr. Mala Arora is the next speaker. She is the one who was so helpful to me regarding my visa. Now I realize she was not at all a secretary. In fact, she is currently the Chairperson of the Indian College of Obstetricians & Gynecologists (ICOG). So currently she is the most important ob-gyn doctor in all of India.

After her talk, I give my second talk, and then follow again lots and lots of great questions, and wonderful interaction with these Indian obstetricians, from whom I learn a ton. Then we break for lunch, which is just downstairs, in a large common room.

It's a buffet lunch, and I love the food. I do not remember all the different, amazing types of servings, but there was curd semiya (a tasty dish prepared with curd and vermicelli), rasam (South Indian soup, traditionally prepared using tamarind juice as a base, with the addition of tomato, chili pepper, pepper, cumin and other spices as seasonings), white rice, chicken chettinad (chicken cooked in some peppery Chettinad paste laced with coconut and onions), rajtha (yogurt, often referred to as curd, together with raw or cooked vegetables), rice biriyani (rice, Indian spices, vegetables, meat, egg, yogurt and dried fruits), dahl phalak (spinach dish), and a few types of nan bread.

I learn a few more things about India and its culture. 'When your face is filled with joy, you are attractive', is a local saying. 'Nothing is impossible unless you think it is so', again a phrase I heard before, but it's highly used and believed here too.

The last name of people is the father's name. The middle name is the old family name. The first name is chosen, such as 'Dave'. So as I am Vincenzo Berghella, my son here would be called something like Dave Berghella Vincenzo. This at least is the tradition in the south.

In the north the last name is the family name for generations. That is why there are so many Patel's, or Singh's, or Gandhi's.

Mirudhu, Dr G, their son and his wife the pediatrician take me then on a nice tour of their private hospital. It has several floors, it is large, fairly modern, clean, and frankly in many ways much better than most of the hospitals I've visited in the USA or Italy, for example.

The neonatal intensive care unit (NICU) has many beds, ample spaces, modern equipment, and seemingly expert staff neonatologists. We scrub our hands upon its entrance. Here the youngest neonates they can keep alive are those born around 26 weeks. That is not bad at all for 2017. Mexico City, as an example, has the same standard. The limit in the USA currently is about 22-23 weeks.

The incidence of breastfeeding is about 100%. It's culturally widely supported, and obviously saves money and lives. My colleagues tell me women breastfeed for at least six months.

About 60% of women in labor in this hospital ask and receive an epidural. That is much higher than most other countries, and probably I guess than over 90% of Indian births. This is a sign of course of a higher-end clientele. There are many different kinds of rooms, all private, all for a fee. The cheapest are about $50/night.

We get to the roof top of the hospital. I enjoy the 360 degrees views of Coimbatore around us. At about six floors, we are the tallest building around. Most structures are one story high. Most buildings are painted white. Some are more modern, and 3-4 stories high.

Many parts of town are still undeveloped, with trees or scrubby vegetation, seemingly unkept, still present. The parking lot for the hospital, right below us on one side, is not paved, just brown soil.

They tell me that as it gets really hot here in the valley in Coimbatore, wealthy people have villas in the hill towns nearby, where the altitude and the green vegetation provide cooler temperature and a relaxing atmosphere.

Interestingly, and certainly news to me, 85% of the hospitals in India have 35 beds or less, and are owed by doctors. Mirudhu and Dr. G's hospital has 100 beds, so it is certainly a big one by Indian standards. They tell me that the fees for care are paid 50% by insurance, versus the other 50% by the patient. Most insurance actually do not cover maternity. Mirudhu and Dr G charge about $1,000 per delivery.

There are about 15 doctors working here. Plus 10 more fellows and then other trainees. There is a dentist, an office for cosmetology, and many other specialists. I would have not have guessed all these services in a maternity hospital.

There are excellent ultrasound machines around, used mostly for fetal sonography. In each ultrasound room, as well as in all public spaces, waiting rooms, offices and bathroom, there are large signs with the national policy regarding not disclosing the fetal gender before birth.

The green sign with white letters on the walls everywhere is clear. "The penalty for doctors performing this test includes rigorous imprisonment up to 3 years and fine of rupees 10,000 ($156)". And that's not all. It continues to say, "For the family members demanding the test the punishment extends up to 5 years of rigorous imprisonment and fine of rupees 50,000 ($783). The pregnant women will not be charged with criminal offense".

As per Census 2016, the population of India is 1.324 billion, comprising 48.5% females and 51.5% males. Therefore, for every 1,000 males in India, there were only about 943 females. Among the States, Kerala had the highest female sex ratio of 1,084 and Haryana has the lowest of 877. These numbers are actually slightly better than they used to be, as the female sex ratio was 927 in 1991 and 933 in 2001.

My ob-gyn colleagues are very adamant about the policy. The person performing the ultrasound looking at the baby during pregnancy cannot absolutely look for fetal gender. One can go to jail for revealing fetal sex anytime during gestation. Her or his license to practice would be taken out. The institution - office, clinic, hospital, etc - where the fetal gender was to be revealed would be closed.

Interestingly, the hospital has even a gym. This was a great idea of Dr G and Mirudhu's son, who manages apparently the hospital so well. Every hospital should have such a wonderful gym. There are many machines to use, not just benches and weights. Everything looks fairly new.

There are 226 FOGSI (The Federation of Obstetric and Gynecological Societies of India) societies. Many of their members attend the All India Congress of Obstetrics and Gynecology (AICOG), held every January for four days.

There is an Indian College of Obstetricians & Gynecologists (ICOG), which is the academic wing of FOGSI with over 770 fellows. It was established by FOGSI on December 21th, 1984 to further promote the education, training, research and knowledge in obstetrics, gynecology and reproductive health.

FOGSI has a Chair, a Vice Chair, a Secretary and 25 board members. Asha says all these appointments are very political, and all these people are very corrupt. She makes it sounds like being appointed to FOGSI makes you a corrupt person, greedy and unethical, by definition. Obviously I have no way to double-check the veracity of her beliefs.

MICOG is the Membership of the Indian College of Obstetricians and Gynaecologists. It works very closely with the MRCOG, that is the Membership of the Royal College of Obstetricians and Gynaecologists. These associations are mostly devoted to certify by national exams obstetricians in India and in the UK, respectively. The Indian medical education and training system is very similar to, and collaborates closely with, the UK system.

The Journal of Obstetrics and Gynecology of India is the official publication of FOGSI. It is published bimonthly and circulated to every individual member. Asha says no good science is published there.

As we leave the Womens Center, I continue to be impressed. This is an oasis of modernism, of wealth, of beautiful rooms, equipment, gardens, waiting rooms, gym equipment. It seemed to me the doctors are fairly well read.

We get driven back to the hotel. My room is really luscious. Fresh fruits, cookies, and chocolates are all waiting for me. All is pristine, the bed is made, all is superclean everywhere. A stark contrast to the true India outside the hotel. I do have some of the chocolates, with those I should be safe in terms of not getting sick.

Late in the afternoon, the plan is for a visit to a temple. I have no idea initially which one, where, and how. But I love the idea of finally some more tourism. I want to learn as much as I can about India.

After a quick 10-minute break to change in the hotel, Asha and I get in the private van which will take us to IshaYoga. The friendly driver is called Sentil. Like most other drivers, his English is very accented for my ear. But understandable if spoken slowly. But these drivers are extremely pleasant, and prefer to stay quiet and out of the way of the guests.

In the van, again Asha is a wealth of information, about so many issues. Back and forth from one to the other, from serious to less serious, and then back again to a prior issue. An avalanche of words and her own wisdom about India and the world.

The meeting we spoke at the day before costed $30 for registration for the hundreds who came to listen to us. Asha and I discuss also that we should email Mala regarding a list of Indian ob-gyns so they can be offered the discounted membership through the SMFM (our American high-risk pregnancy society) CEO, Matt Granato.

As we drive soon out of Coimbatore, as I look around at the population walking around, I have the strange impression that Hindus here are a bit like Berbers in Algeria, in terms of how they dress - very casual and low key for an Italian like me, and socialize continuously.

The environment that goes through my eyes as we drive out of Coimbatore is mostly poor, with lots of garbage lining the roads, unkept houses, unruly traffic.

On the side of the road, apart from an amazing populace, poor and lively, and many huts and animals, I see at some point Perur Pateeswarar Temple. It is very similar to Kapaleeshwarar temple in Chennai. Perur is a Hindu temple dedicated to Shiva.

Lord Shiva, known as 'Patteeswarar', is the presiding deity of this temple together with his consort Parvati, who is known as 'Pachainayaki'. The deity is believed to be 'Swayambu Lingam' (self-emerged). The pillars raised in this temple depict the architectural prowess of the Tamil sculptors.

The hundreds of statues are again of so many colors, so many different shapes, so many events are being shown, so much Hindi religion and mythology depicted.

Asha and I then switch to talk about the fact that one has to pay about $150,000 to get into Medical School. That is a lot of money for anyone, in any country in the world. Considering that India's per capita annual income was about $2,500 in 2013, ranked at 112th out of 164 countries by the World Bank, $150,000 seems like a huge sum, which must ensure only the very rich can have their kids become doctors. In addition, the training to become doctor is long and difficult. It is very challenging to become a doctor in India.

Asha tells me that Sadguru Vasudev, the guru whose temple we are going to visit, started IshaYoga. Jaggi Vasudev was born on September 3rd, 1957, and is commonly known as Sadhguru. He is the Indian yogi and mystic who founded the Isha Foundation, a non-profit organization which offers Yoga programs around the world and is involved in social outreach, education and environmental initiatives. The foundation works in tandem with International bodies like the Economic and Social Council of the United Nations.

He was conferred the Padma Vibhushan award by the Government of India on April 13th, 2017 in recognition of his contribution towards spirituality. Now we are driving to the IshaYoga Center, near Coimbatore. It was founded in 1993, and hosts a series of programs to heighten self-awareness through Yoga.

Yoga, a Sanskrit word, is a group of physical, mental, and spiritual practices or disciplines which originated here in ancient India. There is a broad variety of yoga schools, practices, and goals in Hinduism, Buddhism, and Jainism. Yoga means merging with the god inside of you.

The origins of yoga have been speculated to date back to around the sixth and fifth centuries BCE. Yoga gurus from India later introduced yoga to the West, following the success of Swami Vivekananda in the late 19th and early 20th century.

In the 1980s, yoga became popular as a system of physical exercise across the Western world. Yoga in Indian traditions, however, is more than physical exercise; it has a meditative and spiritual core. One of the six major orthodox schools of Hinduism is also called Yoga, which has its own epistemology and metaphysics, and is closely related to Hindu Samkhya philosophy.

I love to find out where the etymology (origin) of words comes from. In Sanskrit, the word yoga comes from the root yuj which means 'to add', 'to join', 'to unite', or 'to attach' (to yoke).

By figurative extension from the yoking or harnessing of oxen or horses, the word yoga took on broader meanings such as 'employment, use, application, performance'. There are very many compound words containing yoga in Sanskrit. Yoga can take on meanings such as 'connection', 'contact', 'union'.

Many studies have tried to determine the effectiveness of yoga as a complementary intervention for cancer, schizophrenia, asthma, and heart disease. The results of these studies have been mixed and inconclusive. Our research team at Jefferson is currently studying the effect of yoga in pregnancy.

Asha tells me that there are 82 types of yogas. She says yoga is supposed to help bring out the divinity in you. It highlights the futility of many things which upset you.

There is a Yoga of chanting, a Yoga of knowledge, and many more. IshaYoga is a meditation yoga and exercise yoga, a mix. Gurus – such as Sadguru Vasudev - teach the yoga.

While Asha is telling me all this, we risk our life many times on the car, which zips first by traffic in Coimbatore, and then through tiny roads really big enough just for one car but always two-ways. Passing is a gamble with death a serious possibility at every overtaking.

I am fascinated by what I see outside the widow of the van. We drive for almost an hour I think, even if I have little concept of time, as I am so concentrated on the lessons Asha is giving me on so many subjects. There are people everywhere, even in rural areas.

The country side is also very alive. First, the vegetation is lush, tropical, almost jungle-like in some areas. And despite that, there are Indians everywhere, not only dangerously on the side of the street with no sidewalks and our car zipping by.

Most men wear a 'lungi' scarf around their hips as gown. The lungi is a type of sarong and a traditional garment worn around the waist in India, Bangladesh, Pakistan, Somaliland, Nepal, Cambodia, Djibouti, Myanmar and Thailand. It is particularly popular in regions where the heat and humidity create an unpleasant climate for trousers.

For most men I see along the way, this scarf, usually a dirty white, is the only thing they wear. No hat, nothing on their upper body, no shoes or socks. The lungi is used as it's easy to take out when Indians go into the water. It is just a scarf, masterfully wrapped around they waist area and private parts.

My simple Western mind thinks that the scarf could come undo any second. It looks like it's so loosely wrapped. For daily purposes, a simple 'double twist' knot is most popular, where two points in the upper edge of lungi are brought together and twisted around twice, with the ends tucked in at the waist. There are no pins or anything else one can see to keep them on the fragile thin bodies. Moreover, these Indians have no belly to hold this scarf on their waist.

Yoga and meditation help answer the biggest question in life, Who am I? Yoga helps us to try to be balanced. Neither too happy nor too sad.

We have almost arrived now. I see a billboard on the road with Sadguru Vasudev's face on it. It's huge. His face alone is probably thirty feet tall. Of course he looks like the quintessential guru.

Long white beard. Huge white mustaches. Even his eyebrows are mostly white, to emphasize age and wisdom. His eyes are black as opal, penetrating, but so so warm. He has the faintest of smiles, almost like he has captured the secret of life, of true happiness, and is ready to share it with me.

He has his hands in front of his chest, palms joined in a prayer pose, with his eyes looking down. The billboard reads, 'May you unfold your being with folded hands.'

Then Asha points to what looks to me like a forest, just lots of trees. In the middle of it, hard to discern as it's dusk, she points to the head of a statue. It must be huge, as it's peeking through the tall trees.

Jaggi Vasudev designed the 112-foot statue of Adiyogi, which is located kind of near the entrance of the IshaYoga Center. The statue depicts the first yogi (practitioner of yoga). It was inaugurated on Mahashivaratri (a Hindu festival celebrated annually in honor of Shiva), February 24th, 2017 (just 5 months ago!!), by the Prime Minister of India, Narendra Modi.

The Adiyogi statue depicts Shiva (Shiva Linga) as the first yogi or Adiyogi, and first Guru or Adi Guru, who offered yoga to humanity. The statue weighs around 500 tons. The Adiyogi Shiva Statue has been recognized as the 'Largest Bust Sculpture' by the Guinness World Records.

Jaggi Vasudev notes that the statue is for inspiring people to take up yoga. The Ministry of Tourism of the Government of India has included the consecration of the statue in its official Incredible India campaign as a destination.

Sadhguru also said that the height represents the 112 chakras in the human system. Chakras are any center of the body believed to be a psychic-energy center in the esoteric traditions of Indian religions.

Sadhguru notes that the statue is named as 'Adiyogi', which means 'the first yogi', as Shiva is known as the originator of yoga.

The South-facing Adiyogi is also called Dakshinamurthy and Adi Guru (first Guru). The huge head of the Adiyogi statue has a moon on top of it. And there is also a snake around the head.

The foothills of the Velliangiri mountains, forty kilometers from the city of Coimbatore in South India, serve as home for the IshaYoga Center. The Center is dedicated to fostering inner transformation and creating an established state of wellbeing in individuals.

At the temple we get dropped off by our driver. The entrance has a huge arch one goes through. A big cobra is on the central column, probably 30 feet tall. Almost immediately after the entrance, shoes have to come off. Many people do not wear shoes in India anyway to start with.

The stone pavement feels good under my feet. It's almost dark now, but the smooth stones we walk over still have a little bit of the heat from the sun, which just dove under the hills, and so this heat keeps my feet warm.

The temperature is perfect; it must be in the low 70's. All around only Indians. I do not see any Westerners I can discern. I feel like I'm in a Discovery Channel special. In a wonderful remote place.

A bit further in, Asha says we have to leave all our bags, cameras, and iPhones. I am surprised, and worried a bit. For many reasons. We are in the middle of nowhere. Everyone is super poor. Will I ever get my things back?

Mostly, I do not want to part from my iPhone, where I'm recording this amazing trip by writing notes continuously. How will I remember now all I see? Asha tries to bargain for us, but there is no way around this. And after all... we are in the center of the world for meditation and yoga: an iPhone would really be the ultimate snub.

They put our belongings in a yellow bag, with no special sign, and add it to the other thousands they have collected. I have very little hope I'll ever have my iPhone back. I feel bad I'll lose all I've written on this trip. There is no way they'll identify which one is our bag.

Well... there is no other way. I feel relieved from anxieties already. I take it with nonchalance. I'm going to enjoy this place, no worries on my mind. Let yourself go and be happy, I tell myself. India is getting into my blood and my mind and my heart.

The place is truly immense. One can easily get lost. All is grandiose. Asha says this was all built by donations to this guru. The focal point is the Isha Yoga Center. This large residential facility houses an active international community of brahmacharis, full-time volunteers and visitors. Established by Sadhguru as a powerful sthana (a center for inner growth), it is unique in its offering of all the four main paths of yoga - gnana (knowledge), karma (action), kriya (energy) and bhakti (devotion).

One cannot do bad Karma and expect good results, says Asha. Karma means that your actions determine your future. One needs to control the negative experiences.

The center houses the architecturally distinctive Spanda Hall and garden, a 64,000 sq. ft. meditation hall and program facility that is the venue for many residential programs catering to various groups.

The first place to visit is the Nandi - a large metal sculpture of a bull, reclining in a posture that is simultaneously relaxed and alert. Nandi is considered Shiva's cow, according to Asha. This in a way represents the qualities needed to enjoy meditation. One can ring on the bells hanging around its neck before heading off to the next spot to visit.

At the audio/visual center you can enjoy a short introductory video which will give you a better idea of the temple, its background and history. The video is played alternately in both Tamil - the local language, and in English.

You can then begin a short walk around the Outer Parikrama of the Temple Complex. This is a circular path which runs around the main temple - the Dhyanalinga Yogic Temple. The Outer Parikrama incorporates several mystical and aesthetic elements.

The monolithic Trimurthi Panel located behind the Dhyanalinga dome depicts the three fundamental qualities essential for a human being's inner growth: Rudra, Hara and Sadashiva. Rudra is an intense state of mind, Hara is the quality of childlike meditativeness and Sadashiva is an ever blissful state of being.

Right opposite the Trimurthi Panel and adjacent to the IshaYoga Center is the Linga Bhairavi Temple which represents the Divine in its feminine manifestation. Located to the southwest of the Dhyanalinga Temple complex, this deity is unique in that it is in the shape of a linga. The Linga Bhairavi is focused on enhancing the physicality - the material well-being and health of an individual.

Asha says that no matter where life leads you, you must focus on the divine. The head can look away, but the eyes should focus on Shiva. There are birds chirping peacefully. Asha points to Shakti, the Indian god of strength. Shakti is the concept or personification of divine feminine creative power, sometimes referred to as "The Great Divine Mother" in Hinduism.

We walk to, at the northern end, the Theerthakund, a water body embedded 35 feet in the earth, framed by gigantic granite stones and vaulted by a colorful traditional mural depicting the Maha Kumbh Mela. This is a mass Hindu pilgrimage of faith in which Hindus gather to bathe in a sacred or holy river, held every 144 years.

Even this late in the evening, it's past 7pm and dark outside, there are 4-5 people bathing in the sacred waters. They are mostly middle-age men, wearing only something around their private parts, meditating in the large pool.

Asha and I sit down to enjoy the magic of the place. I think I want to go so badly into the waters. But I know we have a lot more to see before this place closes at 8pm. And Asha would freak out probably if I jumped in the pool. Plus, I'm not even sure I'm allowed.

Clearly, if it were just up to me, I would jump in and fully enjoy Theerthakund. A bath in its vibrant cool waters is said to be a preparatory tool to entering the Dhyanalinga and greatly enhances spiritual receptivity while having an uplifting effect on one's physical and mental well-being.

Unlike many temples in India where individuals from foreign countries are not allowed in, the Linga Bhairavi and Dhyanalinga Temples are open to all irrespective of nationality or religion. You can also make several offerings or Arpanas to the Devi on days that are of special significance to them such as the Netra Arpana, which makes a plea to Devi to fulfill desires and wishes.

The Devi Abhaya Sutra is a specially consecrated thread which when tied around the wrist is supportive of one's ambitions and helps in removing fear or the Samarpanam which enhances general wellbeing for a person and their family.

The Yoga Center contains the Dhyanalinga, a unique and powerful energy-form, representing the distilled essence of yogic sciences. It sits under a dome structure as well as Theerthakund, a sacred underground water body. Every week, thousands of people converge at this unique meditation center to seek out inner peace and wellbeing.

In Sanskrit, dhyana means meditation and linga means form. The Dhyanalinga offers a unique meditative space that does not ascribe to any particular faith or belief system, nor does require any rituals, prayers, or worship.

With the sculptural reliefs and symbols of Hinduism, Islam, Christianity, Jainism, Taoism, Zoroastrianism, Judaism, Buddhism and Shinto inscribed on a colossal pillar (the Sarva Dharma Sthamba) located at the front entrance, the Dhyanalinga functions as an icon of singularity, bearing a message of universal welcome.

The Dhyanalinga Yogic Temple is said to be the first of its kind to be completed in over 2,000 years. It was consecrated in 1999 by Sadhguru, does not ascribe to any particular faith and is open to all irrespective of their religion or nationality.

The Inner Parikrama is the intricate pathway leading to the Dhyanalinga Temple. The first element that you encounter is the 17 foot white granite monolith, the Sarva Dharma Stambha.

Symbols of nine major religions of the world are inscribed on three sides of this Stambha as a sign of welcome for one and all beyond religious divide.

After crossing the Stambha, you enter the Inner Parikrama. On the left is the statue of Patanjali, regarded as the father of yogic sciences. On the right is the Vanashree shrine, the feminine deity of the Dhyanalinga temple. Six artistically sculptured granite panels cover the aisles, illustrating the stories of six South Indian sages who attained enlightenment.

Each panel captures a moment in these extraordinary lives. The Parikrama ends at a vaulted tunnel that leads to the dome of the Dhyanalinga. The earthy colors, the natural granite, the attention to details and the shapes that form the Dhyanalinga temple create a warm and esoteric ambiance.

The elliptical Dhyanalinga dome that houses the linga itself is 76 feet in diameter and 33 feet high. It is a pillarless 250,000 brick structure and was built with mud mortar stabilized with lime, sand, alum and herbal additives without the use of any steel, cement, or concrete.

The technology used is this - all the bricks are trying to fall down at the same time but the way they are aligned and balanced ensures they can never fall. This design is similar to that of Roman arch bridges where the keystone ensures the stability of the bridge. The nature of this design ensures a lifespan of at least 5,000 years for the dome. The natural draught of air and the choice of natural materials make the dome a cool and soothing space.

The Dhyanalinga offers a unique set of activities throughout the year aimed at creating and promoting universal values and religious harmony. Daily activities include non-lyrical chants, offered by a talented group of singers, originating from various countries and cultures. These chants allow one to become more receptive to the meditative quality of the space.

As Sadhguru himself says, just sitting silently for a few minutes within the sphere of Dhyanalinga is enough to make even those unaware of introspection experience a state of deep meditativeness.

In fact, the place feels magical from the moment we walk in it. Under the dome, there is an immense circular room. It feels we are in a pagoda. There are flowers everywhere. There are hundreds of lights, but the ambience is not bright, it is a silky dark red. Incense perfumes the charmed air.

As we walk in, some Indians are prostrated face down on the floor, praying. In the middle there is a circular structure, with a large phallic pillar in the middle. Measuring 13 feet 9 inches, the Dhyanalinga is the largest mercury-based linga in the world.

All around the perimeter, along the circular wall, there are small little spaces carved into the stone. Like fireplaces. Asha guides me into one of them, and she goes into another one. I have to scooch down to fit in, as these were not made for 6 feet 2.5 inches tall men.

Once inside, protected around by three walls, I am able to squat and see in front of me the beauty of the Dhyanalinga. I start enjoying the mysticism of the place. I easily fall into a state of calmness, of grace. My mind starts wondering, free.

I think about my life, my loved ones, the meaning of it all, how small and seemingly worthless each of us appears to be, but also what a wonderful opportunity we have been given to live our lives and contribute to others' happiness and the world's wellbeing.

In this tiny cubicle at Dhyanalinga, I definitively live one of those magic moments that are unforgettable in life, and make it all worth it. We should all enjoy such moments as often as we can, be thankful for what we have, strive to be helpful to others as much as possible, and smile.

Also located at the Yoga Center are the Isha Rejuvenation Center and Isha Home School. The Vanaprastha accommodation on the premises was designed to give people with families the opportunity to come and be involved with the center.

Every week, thousands of people converge at the center to seek out inner peace and wellbeing, making it a vibrant hub of spiritual growth and activity. Amazingly, over 28 million new trees have been planted here by two million volunteers. Lots of money pours in this place from devotees around the whole world.

We head back towards the entrance. Before that, we have to pick up our bags and belongings, if they are still there, and especially if they can be found among the thousands. On our walk back, we pass by a couple of food shops, which appear closed.

Right in front of these, Isha Shoppe is the Yoga Center's in-house store where you can purchase Sadhguru's books, CDs and DVDs in English, Tamil, Kannada, Telugu, Malayalam and Hindi. Jaggi Vasudev is the author of several books, including Inner Engineering: A Yogi's Guide to Joy which became best seller of The Washington Post and the New York Times.

Asha and I begin to look at the various books. I am very tempted to buy one, but I do not in the end, as I figure it would be hard to carry the book with me for the rest of this India trip, and I should be able to buy one on Amazon anytime I want when I get back home.

All these books and CDs are on an outside stand, manned by two nice local men. The Shoppe also comprises an inside part, which features eco-friendly products such as woodwork, bags and stone carvings. Organic fiber clothes such as T-shirts, tops and pants can also be purchased here, as well as incense sticks, and yoga mats.

Asha tries to go in this larger covered inside part of the Isha Shoppe, but the door is closed. The two gentle men tell her the shop closes at 8pm. Asha says, 'But it is 7:55pm...' The men kindly tell her there is just no way in, the shop is closed for good for tonight.

To my amazement, Asha keeps on deliberating the fact that it's not 8pm, that she really wants to go in and buy something, that it is absurd they are not letting her in, etc. She shows the men money, arguing she will never be there again, etc etc.

While the men reply in the predictable calmness that characterizes this whole place, Asha instead takes a Western arguing style, debating the fairness, discussing absurd ways to change the men's minds, disputing their peaceful and composed replies.

Ah… sometimes I think we have lost completely priorities in our Western cultures. Sorry Asha, but I am glad that despite 15 minutes of contention, the men never loose they cool, never give in, and never open the shop.

Amazingly, we do recover successfully our bags at the place where we left them a couple of hours ago. Over 90% of the other bags that were there before are gone, and the service people here find ours with surprising ease. There is even still the iPhone in my bag.

As we walk out, I try to take in more of the place, which I do not want to leave. Or at least I want to carry as much of this place inside of me as I can. The air entering my nostrils seems different here, more pure. In this perfect temperature, the dusk now seems magical. The dim atmosphere helps even more to meditate. We all should stop more often and meditate, as to enjoy the simple things in life.

It's a bit past 8pm. Both Asha and I have an appetite. The van driver meets us at the exit, and he is clearly eager to get back. I understand that in general he takes people to tour here much earlier in the day, and he is home in time for dinner with the family.

Asha though begs him to wait just as little bit, as there is an open air restaurant right near the entrance of the IshaYoga Center. We venture in. The place is quite a site. Over a hundred Indians are sitting down in cheap tables and chairs, enjoying the local simple food, sort of an Indian fast food place for the masses.

All looks delicious. Curry and spices smell fill the place despite the fact that there is a roof on our heads, but no walls around the restaurant. Many customers give us the thumbs up or other signs of universal approval as we look in their plates.

Interestingly, the term 'curry', so linked to Indian food, has its origins here in South India. It comes from the Tamil word 'kari', which simply means 'sauce'.

Asha goes to the counter and orders something. It does take a while given the amount of people here, and the inexistence of any organized line. I am so afraid of getting sick from the food - mostly prepared with bare hands, and eaten with bare hands too - that I decline Asha's kind offer to get me a meal.

Finally we get back to the van and our driver, who is not super happy. Asha apologizes. The ride back is enchanting. The narrow road is lined by lights of small shops and food stands, seemingly all always open. Indians buss in and out of them slowly, often in family packs.

While it's past 8:30pm, there is a lot of life outside the homes. I compare this to the downtown of many US cities, big and small, where there is not much life once people go home after work. Here I feel like in a busy beehive, with activities everywhere, and much serenity, happiness.

Community life is the best. It seems like the Indian understood millennia ago that the simple things in life are free: love, friendship, spending quality time socially, good simple healthy food and drink, a shelter for the family unit.

I think of all the wealth in the West, and all the unhappiness and stress. I never meet an anxious person in India. Here in this rural road, so packed alongside it with poor but happy Indians, I think the most happiness must reside. At least as seen from along my air-conditioned van.

Asha of course talks non-stop during the whole ride, and gives me a lot more information about everything India. She says the best human condition is that of being awake with all the senses shut off. To illustrate this, she tells me about Valmiki sage.

Valmiki was born as Agni Sharma to a brahmin named Pracheta (also known as Sumali) of Bhrigu gotra. According to legend he once met the great sage Narada and had a discourse with him on his duties. Moved by Narada's words, Valmiki began to perform penance and chanted the word 'Mara' which means 'to die'.

Agni Sharma performed his penance for several years. He became the 'Rama' of his times (a word similar to 'mara' which he kept on saying), the name of Lord Vishnu. Huge anthills formed around Agni Sharma and this earned him the name of Valmiki.

Asha said he meditated so deeply, he was so removed from the world and anything exterior to him, that the ants eventually covered everything in his body except his head, without him ever noticing. Agni Sharma, rechristened as Valmiki, learnt the scriptures from Narada and became the foremost of ascetics, revered by everyone. He achieved the highest state of meditation and became a saint.

As we zip with the van through the countryside around Coimbatore, there are houses everywhere, people everywhere. Asha tells me now about Vibhuti. Vibhuti is the white sacred ash made of burnt dried wood in Agamic rituals. Hindu devotees apply vibhuti traditionally as three horizontal lines across the forehead and other parts of the body to honor Shiva. Vibhuti smeared across the forehead to the end of both eyebrows is called Tripundra.

Shiva, while he was meditating in the Himalayas, was covered by white ash. The ash is also meant to remind us that we are ash and we go back to ash. It's interesting that ash is so important in Hindi. I of course know all about ash and Christianity. We also say we are ash and will return to ash.

We Christians have the custom of Ash Wednesday. This is when we have black ash placed on our forehead by a priest in a religious service, at the start of the forty days of Lent. The ash is a sign of one's sins and penance. It is an acknowledgment of mortality.

I remember on a plane New York-Rome, I sat near an Indian Catholic priest, who was very excited to go to study theology at the Vatican for a year. I was curious, and asked if there were many Catholics in India. He told me, 'Only about 3% of Indians are Catholics. But that means there are almost 40 million Indian

Catholics.' Considering in Italy there are less than 60 million people, the difference between the numbers of Catholics in India vs Italy is minimal! Amazing.

It's interestingly like we all have ash in our foreheads in both Christianity and Hinduism. I wonder who started first... Probably Hinduism... we put it in the same part of our foreheads, between eyebrows, and generally for similar reasons... also in display for other to know.

Asha then goes on to tell me about the Ganges river and Hinduism. In Hinduism, the river Ganges is considered sacred and is personified as the goddess Ganga. Ganges is the British name for the river, Ganga the Indian name.

Ganga is worshiped by Hindus who believe that bathing in the river causes the remission of sins and facilitates Moksha (liberation from the cycle of life and death), as the water of the Ganges is considered very pure. Pilgrims immerse the ashes of their kin in the Ganges, which is considered by them to bring the spirits closer to moksha. In Hinduism, moksha is the liberation from the cycle of life and death.

Ganga is described as the melodious, the fortunate, the cow that gives much milk, the eternally pure, the delightful, the body that is full of fish, affords delight to the eye and leaps over mountains in sport, the bedding that bestows water and happiness, and the friend or benefactor of all that lives.

There are of course many legends on the Ganges and on Ganga. Bhagavata Purana depicts the birth of the narmad. According to the text, Lord Vishnu in one of his incarnations appeared as Vaman in the sacrificial arena of Asur King Mahabali.

Then in order to measure the universe, he extended his left foot to the end of the universe and pierced a hole in its covering with the nail of his big toe. Through the hole, the pure water of the Causal Ocean (Divine Brahm-Water) entered this universe as the Ganges River.

Having washed the lotus feet of the Lord, which are covered with reddish saffron, the water of the Ganges acquired a very beautiful pink color. Because the Ganges directly touches the lotus feet of Lord Vishnu (Narayana) before descending within this universe, it is known as Bhagavat-Padi or Vishnupadi which means Emanating from the lotus feet of Bhagavan (God).

Ganga finally settles in Brahmaloka or Brahmapura, abode of Lord Brahma before descending to planet Earth at the request of Bhagiratha and held safely by Lord Shiva on his head to prevent destruction of Bhumi Devi (Mother Earth). Then, the Ganges was released from Lord Shiva's hair to meet the needs of the country according to Hindu mythology.

Several years later, a king named Sagara magically acquired sixty thousand sons. One day, King Sagara performed a ritual of worship for the good of the kingdom. One of the integral parts of the ritual was a horse, which was stolen by the jealous Indra.

Sagara sent all his sons all over the earth to search for the horse. They found it in the nether-world (underworld) next to a meditating sage Kapil tied by Lord Indra (the king of Swarg). Believing that the sage had stolen the horse, they hurled insults at him. The sage opened his eyes for the first time in several years and looked at the sons of Sagara. With this glance, all sixty thousand were burnt to death.

The souls of the sons of Sagara wandered as ghosts since their final rites had not been performed. For the moksha of all the sons of Sagara, Anshuman (nephew of those 60,000 sons) started to pray Brahma to bring Ganga to the earth until the end of his life, but was not successful.

Then his son Dilip did the same but did not succeed. When Bhagiratha (which means, 'one who does great hard work' - he got his name from his great hard work for bringing Ganga to earth), one of the descendants of Sagara, son of Dilip, learnt of this fate, he vowed to bring Ganga down to Earth so that her waters could cleanse their souls and release them to heaven.

Bhagiratha prayed to Brahma that Ganga come down to Earth. Brahma agreed and he ordered Ganga to go down to the Earth and then on to the nether regions so that the souls of

Bhagiratha's ancestors would be able to go to heaven. Ganga felt that this was insulting and decided to sweep the whole Earth away as she fell from the heavens. Alarmed, Bhagiratha prayed to Shiva that he break up Ganga's descent.

Ganga arrogantly fell on Shiva's head. But Shiva calmly trapped her in his hair and let her out in small streams. The touch of Shiva further sanctified Ganga. As Ganga travelled to the nether-worlds, she created a different stream to remain on Earth to help purify unfortunate souls there. She is the only river to follow from all the three worlds – Swarga (heaven), Prithvi (Earth) and Patala (netherworld or hell). Thus it is called Tripathaga (one who travels the three worlds) in Sanskrit language.

Because of Bhagiratha's efforts, Ganga descended to Earth and hence the river is also known as Bhagirathi and the term Bhagirath prayatna is used to describe valiant efforts or difficult achievements.

Another name that Ganga is known by is Jahnavi. Story has it that once Ganga came down to Earth, on her way to Bhagiratha, her rushing waters created turbulence and destroyed the fields and the sadhana of a sage called Jahnu.

He was angered by this and drank up all of Ganga's waters. Upon this, the Gods prayed to Jahnu to release Ganga so that she could proceed on her mission. Pleased with their prayers, Jahnu released Ganga (her waters) from his ears. Hence the name Jahnavi (daughter of Jahnu) for Ganga.

It is sometimes believed that the river will finally dry up at the end of Kali Yuga, the last of the four stages the world goes through as part of the cycle of yugas (the era of darkness, the current era) just as with the Sarasvati river and this era will end. Next in (cyclic) order will be the Satya Yuga or the era of Truth.

Asha goes on to tell me about the five vices for Hinduism: attraction/lust, desire/attachment, fear, sadness, anger. Fear means the fear of losing it. Anger is the pain of detachment. All are towards an external object. And we know Hinduism is all about the importance of what is inside of us, not what is outside.

In fact, in Hindu theology, Arishadvarga are the six passions of mind or desire: kama (lust), krodha (anger), lobh (greed), moha (attachment), mada (pride), and matsarya (jealousy). There are the negative characteristics of which prevent man from attaining moksha or salvation.

These are the fundamental tenets of Kali Yuga. The more each individual fights them, the longer will be the life of Dharma in this yuga. Let's list them again:

kama — lust
krodha — anger
lobh — greed
moha — delusory emotional attachment or temptation
mada — pride, hubris
matsarya — envy, jealousy

According to the Hindu scriptures, kama and krodha or lust and anger are responsible for all kinds of difficult experiences which we have in our lives.

With mada or ahankar, the false ego up and active, all our acting in the world becomes selfish. Hence there is no other factor causing the illusory duality of differentiating between 'us' and 'them' and the repeated pain and delusion it entails than the psychological ego-sense.

When the materially identified ego has sided with the materialistic forces of creation (Maya), it is said to have the following faults: kama, krodha, lobha, moha, mada and matsarya. Also called evil passions, man's spiritual heritage constantly gets looted by these internal thieves (and their numerous variations), causing him to lose knowledge of his True Being.

If a person is virtually a prisoner of arishadvargas (the six internal enemies of kama, krodha, lobha, moha, mada and matsarya), then his life is totally governed by the destiny. As a person moves ahead on the path of Self-Realization, the grip of the destiny over him loosens and he gets more and more leverage to change his destiny.

When a person identifies himself with the Self, then he becomes part of the destiny power. His power of mere sankalpa is good enough to materialize and change any situation either for good or bad according to his sankalpa.

Through bhakti and renunciation, these six vices can be overcome. The great Vaishnava Saint Chaitanya Mahaprabhu exhorted, 'Krishna Nama Sankirtan' i.e. the constant chanting of the Lord's name is the supreme healer in Kali Yuga. It destroys sins and purifies the hearts through Bhakti and ensures universal peace.

Asha then goes on to tell me about Buddha. She tells me he was a very lustful man, drinking all the time, with lots of women. He was a prince, very rich, and grew up as a spoiled brat.

At the age of 29, Siddhartha (Siddhartha Gautama is another name for Buddha) left his palace to meet his subjects. Despite his father's efforts to hide from him the sick, aged and suffering, Siddhartha was said to have seen an old man.

When his charioteer Channa explained to him that all people grew old, he discovered aging. The prince then went on further trips beyond the palace. On these he encountered a diseased man, and he discovered sickness. Then he saw a decaying corpse, and he discovered death.

These encounters impressed him, and changed him completely. Buddha left his wife and child. He left his palace and riches. From then on, he strove to overcome ageing, sickness, and death by living the life of an ascetic. I did not know about Buddha and India, and I was surprised we were talking about Buddha here in the subcontinent.

Then Asha goes on to tell me about Bodh Gaya. Bodh Gaya is a religious site and place of pilgrimage associated with the Mahabodhi Temple Complex in the Gaya district in the Indian state of Bihar, in the North-East of India.

Bodh Gaya is famous as it is the place where Gautama Buddha is said to have obtained Enlightenment (bodhi) under what became known as the Bodhi Tree. Buddha meditated under this now epic tree.

For Buddhists, Bodh Gaya is the most important of the main four pilgrimage sites related to the life of Gautama Buddha, the other three being Kushinagar, Lumbini, and Sarnath. In 2002, Mahabodhi Temple, located in Bodh Gaya, became a UNESCO World Heritage Site.

Traditionally, Buddha was born in 563 BC in what is now Nepal. As Siddhartha, he renounced his family at the age of 29 in 534 BC and travelled and meditated in search of truth. After practicing self-mortification for six years at Urubela (Buddhagaya) in Gaya, he gave up that practice because it did not give him Vimukthi.

Then he discovered the Noble Eight-fold path without help from anyone and practiced it, and so he attained Buddhatva or enlightenment. Enlightenment is a state of being completely free from lust (raga), hatred (dosa) and delusion (moha). By gaining enlightenment, you enter Nibbana (or Nirvana), in which the final stage is Parinibbana.

At this place, the Buddha was abandoned by the five men who had been his companions of earlier austerities. All they saw was an ordinary man; they mocked his well-nourished appearance. "Here comes the mendicant Gautama", they said, "who has turned away from asceticism. He is certainly not worth our respect".

When they reminded him of his former vows, the Buddha replied, "Austerities only confuse the mind. In the exhaustion and mental stupor to which they lead, one can no longer understand the ordinary things of life, still less the truth that lies beyond the senses. I have given up extremes of either luxury or asceticism. I have discovered the Middle Way". This is the path which is neither easy (a rich prince) nor hard (living in austere conditions practicing self-denial). Hearing this, the five ascetics became his first disciples.

Asha goes on to tell that the Buddha was trying to understand why there are death, old age, and sickness in the world. He was trying to answer the question, Who am I? He eventually felt the release of fear, and achieved moksha - freedom from the attachments of life.

In Hinduism they believe in rebirth, until Nirvana. Nirvana literally means 'blown out', as in an oil lamp. The term 'nirvana' is most commonly associated with Buddhism, and represents its ultimate state of soteriological release and liberation from rebirths in samsara.

In Indian religions, nirvana is synonymous with moksha and mukti. As we said above, moksha is the liberation from the cycle of birth and death through self-knowledge and the eternal connection of Atman (soul, self) and metaphysical Brahman. Moksha is derived from the root muc, which means free, let go, release, liberate; moksha therefore means liberation, freedom, emancipation of the soul.

All Indian religions assert Nirvana to be a state of perfect quietude, freedom, highest happiness, along with it being the liberation from samsara, the repeating cycle of birth, life and death.

However, Buddhist and non-Buddhist traditions describe these terms for liberation differently. In the Buddhist context, nirvana refers to realization of non-self and emptiness, marking the end of rebirth by dispelling the fires that keep the process of rebirth going. Nirvana in Buddhism is the achievement of a stilling mind, of the cessation of desires, and action, unto emptiness.

In Hindu philosophy, Nirvana is the union of or the realization of the identity of Atman with Brahman, depending on the Hindu tradition. Nirvana in post-Buddhist Hindu texts is also 'stilling mind but not inaction' and 'not emptiness', but rather it is the knowledge of true Self (Atman) and the acceptance of its universality and unity with metaphysical Brahman.

Hinduism, goes on Asha, is not contained in one or a series of books, as are other religions. Rather, gurus passed this knowledge by word of mouth over centuries.

The Bhagavad Gita, often referred to as simply the Gita, is a 700-verse Hindu scripture in Sanskrit that is part of the Hindu epic

Mahabharata (chapters 23–40 of the 6th book of Mahabharata). Asha refers to it as the book of the song of the lord.

Hinduism has no special unique place, like Mecca or Medina, or St Peter's. Also, it has not one god, but thousands of them, as each god has a job to do. The idea is that there cannot be one god because there should be more than one teacher, more than one mentor.

Asha then tells me about Parvathi, which she describes as your inner power. Parvati (can be spelled either way) is also the Hindu goddess of fertility, love and devotion; as well as of divine strength and power. Known by many other names, she is the gentle and nurturing aspect of the Hindu goddess Shakti and one of the central deities of the Goddess-oriented Shakta sect.

Parvathi is the mother goddess in Hinduism, and has many attributes and aspects. Each of her aspects is expressed with a different name, giving her over 100 names in regional Hindu stories of India. Along with Lakshmi (goddess of wealth and prosperity) and Saraswati (goddess of knowledge and learning), she forms the trinity of Hindu goddesses (Tridevi).

Parvati is the wife of the Hindu god Shiva - the protector, the destroyer of evil and regenerator of universe and all life. She is the daughter of the mountain king Himavan and queen Mena. Parvati is the mother of Hindu deities Ganesha and Kartikeya. The Puranas also referenced her to be the sister of the god Lord Vishnu and the river-goddess Ganga.

With Shiva, Parvati is a central deity in the Shaiva sect. In Hindu belief, she is the recreative energy and power of Shiva, and she is the cause of a bond that connects all beings and a means of their spiritual release.

In Hindu temples dedicated to her and Shiva, Parvathi is symbolically represented as the argha or yoni – a stylized representation of female genitalia. She is found extensively in ancient Indian literature, and her statues and iconography grace Hindu temples all over South and Southeast Asia.

It's now close to 9pm, and we are getting back to our hotel. Along the route, I'm impressed shops are still open. Piaggio scooters keep on zigzagging around us in the still unruly traffic. This could not be more quintessential India.

We eat dinner at the hotel, as we both have mounted quite an appetite. There is an amazing buffet, with dozens of delicious Indian local choices. As an example, dosa is a type of pancake from the Indian subcontinent, made from a fermented batter. It is somewhat similar to a crepe in appearance. Its main ingredients are rice and black gram. Dosa is a typical part of the South Indian diet and popular all over the Indian subcontinent.

Traditionally, dosa is served hot along with sambar (lentil-based vegetable stew or chowder cooked with a tamarind broth), stuffing of potatoes or paneer (an unaged, fresh, acid-set, non-melting farmer cheese made by curdling heated milk with lemon juice) and chutney (sauce that can include such forms as tomato relish, a ground peanut garnish or a yogurt, cucumber and mint dip). It can be consumed with idli podi (coarse powder mixture of ground dry spices that typically contains dried chilis, urad (bean), chickpea, and sesame seeds) as well.

They also have paneer butter masala (with tomato puree and typical Indian spices), bhindi tamatar (made of bhindi - okra/lady's finger, tomatoes and onions and a few basic spices), chana masala (Punjabi chickpea curry), vegetable biryani (rice with vegetables), steamed rice, dal tadka (yellow dal garnished with tadka – tempering – of garlic, dry red chili and cumin seeds), rasam, urulai roast (a potato dish), vegetable cannelloni (!!), cauliflower manchurian, vegetable hakka noodle (boiled noodles stir fried with sauces and vegetables or meats), malpua (crushed ripe bananas or coconut, flour, and water or milk, deep fried in oil, and served hot), lahori chicken tikka (pre-marinated smokey-flavored grilled chicken), fish finger, shredded lamb in ginger soya sauce, and dozens of different little desserts.

I have a lot of dosa with four different sauces, sambar, as well as nan (leavened, oven-baked flatbread) with tomato chutney.

Heaven. This food is also so digestible. I can never get enough. And I always feel great in the hours after an Indian meal.

Monday July 31, 2017

My alarm goes off in the beautiful hotel room, and I wake up thinking it's the middle of night. I am still tired and jet lagged, but the thought of seeing more of India gets me up happy. I have a regenerating shower in the elegant glass shower room, larger by itself than many bathrooms.

I have a wonderful buffet breakfast in the hotel restaurant. This is the same place as last night, the food was so good, I want to eat here the rest of my life. There is a large tv showing the Indian CNN channel again. Interestingly, they are talking about Sonia Gandhi.

Sonia Gandhi is an Indian politician of Italian descent. Another connection between Italy and India. A member of the Nehru–Gandhi family, she is a former president of the Indian National Congress. Having taken over as the party leader in 1998, seven years after her husband's assassination, she remained in office for a record nineteen years.

Born in a small village near Vicenza, Italy, Sonia was raised in a Roman Catholic Christian family. After completing her primary education at local schools, she moved to Cambridge for higher education and married Rajiv Gandhi in 1968.

She later took up Indian citizenship and began living with her mother-in-law, the then Prime Minister of India, Indira Gandhi, in her New Delhi residence. Indira Gandhi was the daughter of Jawaharlal Nehru, the first Indian prime minister.

Indira Gandhi served as Prime Minister from January 1966 to March 1977 and again from January 1980 until her assassination by two bodyguards in October 1984, making her the second longest-serving Indian prime minister after her father.

Rajiv Gandhi took office after the 1984 assassination of his mother, Prime Minister Indira Gandhi, to become the youngest Indian Prime Minister at the age of 40. Rajiv Gandhi remained Congress President until the elections in 1991. While campaigning for the elections, he was assassinated by a suicide bomber from the Tamil Tigers.

Sonia Gandhi stayed away from the public sphere, even during the years of her husband's premiership. Following her husband's assassination, Gandhi was invited by Congress leaders to take over the government, but she refused and stayed away from politics. She finally agreed to join politics in 1997 after constant prodding from the party; the following year, she was nominated for party president, and elected.

Under her leadership, the Congress went on to form the government after the 2004 elections in coalition with other center-left political parties. Gandhi has been credited for being instrumental in the alliance, which was re-elected to power in 2009. Sonia Gandhi declined the premiership following the 2004 victory, but she led the United Progressive Alliance (UPA) and the National Advisory Council.

Although she never held any public office in the government of India, Gandhi has been widely described as one of the most powerful politicians in the country, and is often listed among the most powerful women in the world.

Continuing the Nehru-Gandhi political dynasty, Rajiv Gandhi and Sonia Gandhi's son Rahul is a Member of Parliament and the current President of the Indian National Congress.

Asha, as usual, pays for all the tips, including a small one for the breakfast. She talks about the severe shortage of rains, and therefore of water, which often plagues India.

Our driver is waiting to take us to Mirudhu and Dr G's hospital again. I would probably rather tour around, but they have all been so nice that I go with the flow.

Nursing homes here are tiny hospitals with 3-10 beds. There are so many of them. While we travel, we see one KFC (Kentucky Fried Chicken), and one McDonald. I'm not happy about it, but thankful also these brands have not (yet) taken over at least here in South India.

Asha actually explains to me that McDonald is expensive, and is considered a food place for rich people. I guess all true Indian food must be so cheap, and good, therefore hard to compete against. Yeah!! McDonald is not popular in India.

Men do not wear wedding bands. Women do. While Asha does not say it, India seems to me to be still very much a male-dominated society, at least in the public sphere. Probably women rule more at home, as in most cultures.

The traffic is intense, as usual. There are cows roaming the streets. I am surprised I never see a crash, but I do witness many close calls.

People, especially women, were dresses which are so beautiful and so colorful. Asha says everywhere in India there is usually lots of night life.

It's wonderful that Asha has absolutely no filter when she talks. Her son lives in Mumbai. She obviously adores him, as every mother adores her son. She is not happy with his girlfriend. I'm sure she would love to scheme something so they would break up. I have heard such talks in so many families, in every culture.

She explains to me that there are four kinds of families in India. The first type is the families in business; she said they do not have much education. Then come the academics families. I assume she thinks her family belongs to this second group, as she is a physician, as are many others in her family.

They third type is the Rajput. This is a caste associated with military careers. The members of these families get educated in defense-related matters. The fourth kind of families, finally, is the worker families, the ones whose members do manual labor.

Asha's son's girlfriend's family is in business. I can tell Asha implies that this is just not good enough for a family of academics like hers. Interestingly, she also tells me that her son in Mumbai works in a company which makes tea; he works in the social branch. I do not see much academics in that job...

Asha says that it is difficult to have success without someone who you know in India to help you. She complains about the corruption in India, and the red tape. To get anything done in India, one has to know the influential people.

This reminds of Italy, which I fled when I was a teenager because it was so non-meritocratic. She speaks like 99% of Italians would. Funny in a way. The world has similar problems everywhere. It seems like in India, as well as Italy, many get ahead because of who they know, not because of talent and effort.

We switch quickly back and forth among different subjects. Whatever comes to mind to Asha, she says it. She states again that maternal mortality has decreased a lot in the last few years in India, going down to 170 women dying of issues related to pregnancy from 400 every 100,000 pregnancies.

Kerala, the state we are near, in the south-east part of India, is a very good state, Asha states. They cultivate and have the best food.

Maternal-Fetal Medicine (MFM) is still lacking in India. She says there is really no concept of MFM. There is one perinatology (synonymous with MFM) fellow in the whole country.

Coimbatore is an industrial town. It is very entrepreneurial. The comparison is often made with Manchester in the U.K., as both Manchester and Coimbatore became famous for their textiles.

We get to the Womens Center. Today there are a lot of people around. There must be over 80 Indians, mostly women, and many babies, in the large main waiting room.

We sit down in Mirudhu's office, and we have over an hour of conversation. This dialogue in a way is the reason for the whole trip. These Indian colleagues want to finally begin to establish a national program for MFM training, based on what we have in the USA. As I have been a leader for both the Society for MFM, and for MFM training, both at national levels, they see me as the perfect expert to lead them into this effort.

At Mirudhu's hospital, they actually do have a 2-year fetal training program, to which now they have added a maternal component, too. This has been possible because of Gopi, who is here with us too. He became the chairman of the ob-gyn board at the state level. Thanks to his administrative and political work, now one can officially become MFM-trained in this state, Tamil Naru.

One of the logistical problems is that many radiologists and neonatologists are doing fetal ultrasound. At this point the subject drifts to the PCPNDT act. The Pre-Conception and Pre-Natal Diagnostic Techniques Act is a 1994 Act of the Parliament of India enacted to stop female feticides and arrest the declining sex ratio in India. The act banned prenatal sex determination.

This act is strictly enforced. Unfortunately, some try to skirt around it. When they do a prenatal ultrasound, they do not say 'male' or 'female'. But they do use other means, such as code words, to inform the couple. For example, by using Friday for males and Monday for females.

Asha is one of six kids. She never stops talking even if there are about eight of us sitting around and having a pleasant conversation in Mirudhu's office.

They discuss a recent case of fetal ventriculomegaly - excess fluid in the head, usually caused by a smaller, often maldeveloped, brain. The charts here are still paper charts, not computerized. Abortions are legal up to 20 weeks of gestation.

The courts take about six weeks to approve a case for abortion after 20 weeks. A recent case in the news was that of an 11year-old girl who was raped but could not terminate the pregnancy because at 32 weeks the courts deemed her to be too far along.

My Indian colleagues tell me that the vast majority of pregnant women here get prenatal care. Once identified as pregnant, women in fact get picked up for free from their homes by state employees so they can go to get their prenatal care visits.

India though is very diverse. Apparently the middle of India does badly. States like Uttar Pradesh, a state in northern India bordering Nepal, are poor.

To become a doctor, it takes about four and a half years of medical school. Then to become an ob-gyn, one has to do one year of internship, and three years of ob-gyn training. In India, the deliveries are for the most part done by doctors, like in the US, and not by midwives, as in many other parts of the world.

Mr. G and his wife Mirudhu take us eventually out to lunch. The best food is that from the nearby state of Kerala, so they take us to a place that has Kerala's food. I feel a bit like I would be in my native Pescara, where fish is king as per food, and friends would take me out instead to a Roman restaurant - Rome is famous more for meats and heartier meals. But I'm excited to try new food. To explore something new. I love that.

The place is clean, neat, modern. Mr. G and Mirudhu's son, who again is the one who manages their hospital, as well as his lovely pregnant wife, who is a pediatrician at the hospital, join us too. Their son married well, I think, as his wife seems to be pleasant, always smiling, smart, and caring. She is probably a great doctor.

The menu is informative. I read that coconut production plays an important role in the economy and culture of Kerala. The state is named after the coconut tree with 'Kera' meaning coconut tree, and 'Alam' meaning land. Keralam = Land of the coconut trees!

At the table next to us, we strike a conversation - Dr G is very extroverted and communicative - with a woman who drove from here in Coimbatore to London. It took her 72 days. She needed 11 visas to go through a lot of countries, including many former USSR states.

The food is delicious. The moily fish is great. This is a Malabar (southern India region) fish curry in a coconut-milk based sauce. It melts in my mouth, and stimulates my taste buds to orgasmic levels. They order several dishes, which we all share, and one is more mouth-watering than the other.

Our conversation switches to many different topics. Indians are not circumcised. The IUD - intrauterine device, used for contraception, is commonly used. Many women get their tubes tied after they finish having babies.

Contraceptive usage has been rising gradually in India. In 1970, 13% of married women used modern contraceptive methods, which rose to 35% by 1997 and 48% by 2009. About three-fourths of these were using female sterilization - the tying of tubes - which is by far the most prevalent birth-control method in India.

India's fertility rate as of 2015, was 2.4 births per woman. The replacement rate, that is the rate of fertility per woman at which the populations stays the same, is approximately 2.1 in most industrialized nations and about 2.5 in developing nations (due to higher mortality). With 26 million births a year, India is still making a lot of babies, and growing in population.

I am impressed Dr G and Mirudhu's daughter-in-law does not know the gender of the 36 week fetus she is carrying. Just amazing. Especially given the access to ultrasound her family has. But I believe them.

They tell me that in India about 50% of people are vegetarians, while the other 50% are not. In the north, people drink alcohol, while that does not happen as much in the south at all. People everywhere drink lots of milk. They think it protects against sickness. There is really no winter in much of India.

Our conversation, so pleasant and interesting, then switches to Indian cinema. Bollywood is such an entrenched part of the culture here. Bollywood, formally known as Hindi cinema, is the Indian Hindi language film industry, based in the city of Mumbai (formerly Bombay), Maharashtra, India.

Bollywood is part of the larger cinema of India (also known as Indywood), which includes other production centers making films in other Indian languages. Linguistically, Bollywood films tend to use a colloquial dialect of Hindi-Urdu, or Hindustani, mutually intelligible to both Hindi and Urdu speakers, while modern Bollywood films also increasingly incorporate elements of Hinglish.

Indian cinema is the world's largest film industry in terms of production, with an annual output of 1,986 feature films as of

2017, and Bollywood is its largest film producer, with 364 Hindi films produced annually as of 2017.

Bollywood represents 43% of Indian net box office revenue, while Telugu and Tamil cinema represent 36%, and the rest of the regional cinema constitute 21%, as of 2014. Bollywood is thus one of the largest centers of film production in the world. In terms of ticket sales, Bollywood sells an estimated 3.6 billion tickets annually across the globe, compared to Hollywood's 2.6 billion tickets sold.

The name 'Bollywood' is a portmanteau derived from Bombay (the former name for Mumbai) and Hollywood (in California), the center of the American film industry. The naming scheme for 'Bollywood' was inspired by 'Tollywood', the name that was used to refer to the cinema of West Bengal.

Dating back to 1932, 'Tollywood' was the earliest Hollywood-inspired name, referring to the Bengali film industry based in Tollygunge (in Calcutta, capital of West Bengal), whose name is reminiscent of 'Hollywood' and was the center of the cinema of India at the time. It was this chance juxtaposition of two pairs of rhyming syllables, Holly and Tolly, that led to the portmanteau name Tollywood being coined.

Here in Tamil Nadu, the film industry is called Kollywood. The movies are in Tamil as a language. All around the table are very proud of Kollywood. Kollywood is a colloquial term being a portmanteau of Kodambakkam (a residential neighborhood in Chennai) and Hollywood.

The Malayalam film industry is called Mollywood. More imaginatively, Bengaluru's Kennada film industry is called Sandalwood.

I finally learn the difference between Hindi, which is the language, and Hindu, which is the religion. I never knew that!

We talk about the Indian philosophy way of life. Somehow the discussion goes then to 'The man who knew infinity,' a movie. The Man Who Knew Infinity is a 2015 British biographical drama film about the Indian mathematician Srinivasa Ramanujan, based on the 1991 book of the same name by Robert Kanigel.

The film stars Dev Patel as Srinivasa Ramanujan, a real-life mathematician who after growing up poor in Madras, India, earns admittance to Cambridge University during World War I, where he becomes a pioneer in mathematical theories with the guidance of his professor, G. H. Hardy, portrayed by Jeremy Irons. I need to watch it as soon as I get back.

Our lunch is just wonderful. I have a sweet dish with fennel seeds and sugar. Delicious. The conversation moves to the fact that there were many U.K. citizens who settled here in South India in large plantations during colonization. Many stayed, and are still around. Obviously over the two centuries of British rule in India there were many babies born to British settlers and Indian locals. They are called Anglo-Indians.

Dr. G says many Anglo-Indians became school teachers and nannies. India is so diverse they say. Northeast Indians for example look Mongolian. In understand now why some people looked so Asian but not Indian in the airport.

It's sad to leave the restaurant. The food was delicious, and the conversation so interesting. It's almost time for me to get to the airport. Asha is staying another couple of days. But Dr G and Mirudhu want to stop at another site before taking me to the airport. My luggage is already in the car, with the trusted driver waiting for us.

In the car, Dr G and his wife Mirudhu tell me they went to the same medical school in Chennai, where they first met. They seem to be a couple who was able to overcome the obvious differences they have, focus on common goals, and use their different strengths to the advantage of their family team.

The traffic is still wonderful to watch. So chaotic and lively. It reminds me a bit of the traffic in Naples, Italy. But here the diversity of things on the road is 100 times more varied. Interestingly, there are many old models of Fiat cars and Piaggio scooters zipping around.

We stop in a market. Some of it is open air, some in a huge hangar-like building. There must be over 80 different stands selling a bit of everything for locals and the occasional tourist. There are statues, paintings, jewelry, textiles, clothes, foods, pottery, carpets, furniture, swings, other household items, shoes, sandals, bags, Hindu religious items, a bit of everything for sale. The colors of all these items are bright, and illuminate the place.

I want to hurry up and make sure I make my plane. I have to take three planes to get back to Rome. Missing one would be a disaster. So I zoom around the stands, looking for something simple, small (to carry in my carry-on), and not too expensive to bring back to my family members when I get back to Italy.

I settle on a stand with many Indian women jewelry. I eventually buy several bracelets, colorful and definitively local. These could not be found anywhere but here in India. I plan to give one to each of some of the women in my life, my nieces, wife, sister, mother.

A short van trip later, I'm dropped off at the Coimbatore airport. The police though stops me right away at entrance. A military guy begins to question me. I hardly understand his English, very mixed with Tamil or some other language I do not understand. He is nice, but stern-looking.

Dr G steps out of the van and comes to rescue me, but he is not needed, as the officer lets me through after checking my documents. At the JetWay airline check-in counter, a nice young attractive Indian lady helps me with boarding passes. After I request it, she checks me all the way to Rome!!!

I did not know, but Jet Airways is a major Indian international full-service airline based in Mumbai. In October 2017, it was the second-largest airline in India after IndiGo with an 17.8% passenger market share.

I am delighted to get already here in Coimbatore the boarding passes for Coimbatore-Chennai, then for Chennai-Dubai, as well as for Dubai-Rome. I can hardly believe my luck. I am so grateful that I ask the JetWay lady how to write a thank you note. She hands me a blank one, I fill it out with hyperbolic gratitude towards her and her company, and hand it back in an envelope. All seems great.

I get to the waiting area, which is small. Coimbatore does not have a big airport. I sit down in a chair that allows me to notice the display with the eight or so flights leaving in the next 6-8 hours. Not a busy airport for sure. The display switches every 20 seconds or so between English and Tamil. The Tamil display is almost funny as it is so unreadable to me.

I notice there is a flight for Chennai - my first destination - leaving now. People are already boarding. I consider jumping on it. I would have to go back though security to the check-in counter to switch my boarding pass. But I think I would look pushy, it might not be feasible both time-wise and rules-wise this late, plus my carry-on was already labeled for the 18:30 (6:30pm) flight.

Plus I have already a comfortable two-hour time interval with the 18:30 flight in Chennai to get in for the 21:45 (9:45pm) flight to Dubai. So I stay put, and wait patiently. I have a lot I can write on my trusted laptop.

I wait patiently, continuously looking at the display. The 18:30 Chennai flight is always on, but the gate is never announced. A couple of flights board while a couple of hours go by.

The clock gets to 18:12 (6:12pm) and there is no boarding yet. I begin to panic. Is the flight being cancelled? I send WhatsApp messages to Asha. She texts me back that Dr G will look into it. I do not know what to do. There seems to be nobody to ask to.

Then I look at my boarding passes. The Coimbatore to Chennai boarding pass says that it's supposed to depart at 19:30 instead of 18:30!! Oh god!! The lady at the check-in counter should have noticed, and told me, and tried to put me on the earlier flight!!

I go and look closer at the departures display. Interestingly, it does not says delayed or anything. But as I look closer, it says under the second tiny column, 'ETD', 19:30!! Oh my...

I'm panicked now. I was already told that in Chennai I have to switch terminals and go from the domestic to the international terminals. Insert baggage checks, passport checks, etc, I might never make it!! This trip to India was not lucky regarding planes; for sure!

Eventually I board this now 19:30 flight from Coimbatore to Chennai. There were for sure no other options. It's a propeller plane again. Sandokan (the character and tv show from the books I used to read when I was a boy) music is being played!!

The stewardess must be from north-east India, as she looks a bit Mongolian. Like the lady at the Radisson Hotel, I think, which I mistook for Chinese or south-east Asian, but in retrospect must have been a north Indian with Mongolian features.

I doze off a bit, helped by the Sandokan soothing music. The stress of waiting for this plane, and worrying about the next ones, has taken a little toll. I sleep only 15 minutes, but I feel regenerated and calmer now. I accept whatever destiny has in store for me during this long trip. I always look at the positive side.

I do not dare eat the sandwich they serve me. I made it so far! I do not want to get sick at the end. And during flights. The sandwich has got mayo probably. And vegetables. Exactly the staff I'm not supposed to eat. The mayo could have old milk, which is the number one reason - according to Dr G - people get sick in India.

I cannot write on the plane, as I am just too wired up regarding not making the next flight. I've made my calculations. They announced a one hour and twenty minute flight. We took off at exactly 7:26pm. So I should arrive at about 8:46pm in Chennai. By 9:00pm I should be off the plane. Then I have only 20 minutes before they close the plane for Dubai at 9:20pm. I probably won't make it. Well...

The issue I guess is always that I yearn to move forward. I love to get to the next thing. I'm supposed to land in Rome on August 1st, 2017 at 7:25am, and spend time with my family, in particular with our two beloved sons Andrea and Pietro. I have not seen Andrea in particular for a while - except for the brief Naples trip.

The captain says we were delayed due to the late arrival of the airplane. And that there will be turbulence on our descent to Chennai. I think Nirvana, Karma, Indian meditation, and relax Vincenzo, just relax. I think of IshiYoga. The warm pavement. The lights. The soothing music. Keeping my third eye on my inner self. I have to pee though!

We land in Chennai. I tell the person next to me that I have a close international connection. I'm in the penultimate row, and manage to get to the very back of the plane, where we'll deboard from. I see the bathroom, ask the stewardess if I can go in, and relive myself quickly.

While doing it, I hear the door of the plane open, and the first words I hear are, "Emirates?? Emirates??!!" Someone is looking out for me! I dart out, saying "I'm Emirates!", and the kind Indian airport officer escorts me to the bus.

He lets a few more people quickly in the bus, and then tells the pilot to take off. I feel bad a bit - about leaving some other passengers behind because this bus is hurrying for me, but happy I have some help to negotiate this airport.

As arrive at the terminal, I'm the first off the bus after the officer. He does not speak much, but tells me to follow him. I'd like to run now! But he signals me with his hand not to, we are walking quickly enough. In less than a minute, we are past baggage claim - no checks whatsoever, and at the exit of this domestic terminal.

I see Geta! And her husband! I had been texted - by Geta, by Asha, and by some unknown number - that a golf cart would be waiting for me to take me quickly to the International Terminal. Indeed, the cart is right there. Gita tells me to jump in, after I give her a kiss and shake her husband's hand.

I seat immediately in the back reversed seat of the golf cart, looking towards the rear, and the driver takes off with my personal airport officer sitting up front with him. As we take off, I wave a kiss to Geta and her husband. I feel bad they came all the way here, and I had only a second to see them.

The driver speeds through people for the next 3-4 minutes, as we cover much ground, which I would have taken much longer to pass through even running with my heavy bag.

We arrive at the International Terminal. I have decided not to look at my iPhone for the time now. No reason to. We just have to get through all the next obstacles ASAP. At the entrance, the officer finds an ingress with no people in line (another one had at least twenty). The stern policeman checks my passport and ticket, and lets me in after ten seconds of interminable checking.

The Emirates check-in booths are in front of us. I figure we do not need them, I already have boarding passes. But my officer states I have to get new boarding passes. I guess I need them to be labeled from Emirates, since the ones I have are from JetWay. Oh well...

There is not much of a line, and I get seen fairly quickly by an alacritous officer. In probably 2-3 minutes, he prints two new boarding passes (I ask for the one for Dubai-Rome, too). He then for a couple of minutes talks with other check-in staff, there seems to be something else I need, I do not understand their Tamil or what is going on... Another few panicked seconds...

But soon my personal officer says to them I can have back my passport and my boarding passes from Emirates, so we can go. Another fifty yards, and we are at passport control. I see the officer separating from me, and pointing ahead. "Aren't you coming with me?" I plead. "No", is his polite short answer. "Go ahead".

Ok, I'm on my own now. But... am I a lucky guy or what? There is nobody in line for passport control!! I get through quickly. Then there is baggage check. Somebody else here seems to know about me. I get in line. Another officer tells me to put my bag and other belongings on the rolling belt. And then get back in the about 10-man-long line. He reassures me, as the other officer had tried to do, that there is no need to rush now. I've made it.

I'm tall, I can see over everyone's heads. Past the baggage check point, I set my eyes on a screen, where I seem to locate the departure information. Near the top, I see 21:45... that is the time of my flight... then next to it finally (after it was shown in Tamil) the word 'Dubai'. And then at the end of this row on the right, 'Security'. Other rows - not for my flight - say 'Boarding'.

Yes! My flight is not even boarding. I've got my flight under control. I'm not at the gate yet, but getting closer. After 10 minutes of a slow line, I'm through baggage claim. I realize the International Terminal at Chennai has just 21 gates. My gate 17 is less than 100 yards past the baggage claim. Now I know for sure I made it. I can relax. I celebrate by going to pee again. It's purely transparent.

My memories of India are magnificent. India, shaped like a diamond, is indeed a jewel of a country. In 4,348 kilometers, I'll be back in Rome, Italy. But man, I will miss India... which is going to stay in my heart and mind the rest of my life.

Acknowledgements

My sincere gratitude to
Asha, Mala, Gita, Mirudhu and Dr G,
as this trip would have not have occurred without your help

www.ingramcontent.com/pod-product-compliance
Lightning Source LLC
LaVergne TN
LVHW011336080426
835513LV00006B/390